Stereotype Killers

The Pornstar Who Never Had Sex, The Emperor Who Refused the Throne, The Billionaire in Basketball Shorts, The Redneck Tech Genius and 45 Lives That Shatter What You Thought You Knew

Dr. Robbie King

Stereotype Killers

The Pornstar Who Never Had Sex, The Emperor Who Refused the Throne, The Billionaire in Basketball Shorts, The Redneck Tech Genius and 45 Lives That Shatter What You Thought You Knew

Stereotype Killers

The Pornstar Who Never Had Sex, The Emperor Who Refused the Throne, The Billionaire in Basketball Shorts, The Redneck Tech Genius and 45 Lives That Shatter What You Thought You Knew

Dr. Robbie King

Copyright © 2025 by Dr. Robbie King and Eaglewolf Wellness, LLC.

Stereotype Killers: The Pornstar Who Never Had Sex, The Emperor Who Refused the Throne, The Billionaire in Basketball Shorts, The Redneck Tech Genius and 45 Lives That Shatter What You Thought You Knew by Dr. Robbie King.

All rights reserved. No part of this publication may be reproduced, distributed, or transmitted in any form or by any means, including photocopying, recording or other electronic or mechanical methods, without the prior written permission of the publisher, except in the case of brief quotations embodied in critical reviews and certain other, non-commercial uses permitted by copyright law.

For permission, requests, write to the publisher, addressed "Attention: Permissions Coordinator" at the address below: Eaglewolf Wellness, LLC, 1680 Michigan Avenue, Suite 700-136, Miami Beach, FL 33139 United States of America.

Ordering Information: Quantity sales. Special discounts are available on quantity purchases by corporations, associations, and others. For details, contact the publisher at the address above.

First Edition, First Printing.

ISBN: 979-8-263-44911-7

Printed in the United States of America
1 2 3 4 5 6 7 8 9 10 30 29 28 27 26 25

"WYSIATI: What you see is all there is. This rule means that people make judgments based only on the information available, without considering what is missing. When information is scarce, our minds construct a coherent story and then treat it as if it were complete."

- Daniel Kahneman, Israeli-American Psychologist and Economist, founder of the science of Behavioral Economics and 2002 Nobel Prize winner in economics.

This book is dedicated N. Life would not have been the same without you. The motivation, the drive, and determination came from the energy you gave me. Thank you.

Stereotype Killers

The Pornstar Who Never Had Sex, The Emperor Who Refused the Throne, The Billionaire in Basketball Shorts, The Redneck Tech Genius and 45 Lives That Shatter What You Thought You Knew

Dr. Robbie King

Table of Contents

1. Introduction: A World of Stereotypes, Archetypes, Prototypes, and Other "Types" 20

2. Chapter 1: Bill Murray - The Fame-Despising Superstar 24

3. Chapter 2: F.W. De Klerk - The Dictator Who Dismantled his Own Regime 28

4. Chapter 3: Tom Selleck - The Super Relaxed Suntanned Smoothie Who Was Actually the Hardest Worker in Hollywood 33

5. Chapter 4: Dr. Hugo Eckener - The Tycoon Who Dismantled His Empire for the Sake of Ethics 37

6. Chapter 5: Ross Perot - The Redneck Tech Genius Who Tried to Save the Republic 42

7. Chapter 6: Barry Goldwater - The Pro-Choice, Pro-Civil Rights, Pro-Minorities, Pro-Labor, Pro-Feminism, Anti-Racist, Pro-LGBTQ+, Pro-Drug, Anti-Religious Fervor, Far-Right Conservative 47

8. Chapter 7: Paul Kruger - The Politician Who Despised Government 52

9. Chapter 8: Bill Goldberg - The Jewish Man Who Looks Like a Harley-Davidson Biker—and Fights Better Than One, Too 56

10. Chapter 9: Rick Harrison - The Historian, Scholar, Pawnbroker, and Guardian of Knowledge 60

11. Chapter 10: Albert Schweitzer - The Man Who Mastered Everything 64

12. Chapter 11: Steve Martin - The Comedian Who Refused to Be One-Dimensional 68

13. Chapter 12: Peter Weller - The 80s Action Hero with a PhD in Renaissance Studies 72

14. Chapter 13: Elvira - The Gothic Valley Girl — Mistress of the Dark, Master of Reinvention 76

15. Chapter 14: Nina Hartley - The Pornstar, Philosopher, Nurse, and Feminist Who Obliterated Every Assumption 80

16. Chapter 15: Cory Everson - The Muscle Stereotype Destroyer — The Woman Who Made Strength Look Beautiful 84

17. Chapter 16: Pandora Peaks - The Pornstar Who Never Had Sex on Camera — The Centered Soul Behind the Centerfold 88

18. Chapter 17: James Randi - The Honest Scientific Magician Educator 92

19. Chapter 18: Rodney Dangerfield - The Extremely Late-Blooming Jewish Comedian Who Got No Respect—Until He Got All of It 96

20. Chapter 19: Tony Danza - The Italian-American Tough Guy — Who Was Also the Kindest Man in the Room 100

21. Chapter 20: Siskel and Ebert - The Non-Pretentious Film Critics — Movies for the People 104

22. Chapter 21: Koos De la Rey - The Self-Educated General Who Defeated History's Greatest Empire 108

23. Chapter 22: Isaac Asimov - The Writer Who Wrote About Everything—Except Cooking 113

24. Chapter 23: John Gierach - The Fisherman, Philosopher, and Henry David Thoreau of the Waters 117

25. Chapter 24: Anatoly Tarasov - The Soviet Innovator Who Transformed Hockey with Ballet, Chess, and Finesse 121

26. Chapter 25: Bill James - The Meatpacking Security Guard Who Revolutionized Baseball Without Ever Setting Foot on the Field 125

27. Chapter 26: Steve Reeves - The Bodybuilder Who Hated Showing Off His Body 129

28. Chapter 27: Sam Walton - The Billionaire Who Drove an Old Truck and Wore Overalls... 132

29. Chapter 28: General George C. Marshall - The Quiet General Who Led the Greatest War in History Without Saying a Word 136

30. Chapter 29: Arnold Schwarzenegger - The Bodybuilder Polymath Who Left Da Vinci Biting the Dust.................. 140

31. Chapter 30: John Bogle - The Saint of Wall Street 145

32. Chapter 31: Mr. Rogers - The Multimillionaire Who Was Also the Nicest Man in the World 149

33. Chapter 32: Bob Ross - The Drill Sergeant Who Chose to Whisper to the World 153

34. Chapter 33: Bob Woodward - The Journalist Who Changed History 157

35. Chapter 34: Ted Koppel - The In-Depth, Ethical Anchorman Who Refused to Sensationalize the News 161

36. Chapter 35: Adam Sandler - The Laid-Back Billionaire in Basketball Shorts and XXXL T-Shirts 165

37. Chapter 36: Neil Armstrong - The Greatest Achievement, the Quietest Man.. 169

38. Chapter 37: Mahatma Gandhi - The Revolutionary Who Defeated an Empire Without Firing a Shot 173

39. Chapter 38: George Washington - The Would-Be Emperor Who Said No to the Throne 177

40. Chapter 39: Colonel Sanders - The Old Man Who Achieved Success Nearing Age 70 181

41. Chapter 40: Dr. Phil - The Sensitive Southern Psychologist... 184

42. Chapter 41: Henry Ford - The Farmer Who Changed the World Forever... 187

43. Chapter 42: Ian Anderson - The Rock Star of Temperance... 190

44. Chapter 43: Rowan Atkinson - The Electrical Engineer Who Made the World Laugh Without Saying a Word..... 194

45. Chapter 44: Harry S. Truman - The Everyman President 197

46. Chapter 45: Jimmy Carter - The President Whose Life of Service Began After the Presidency 201

47. Epilogue: Stereotypes?... Out the Window They Go 205

48. Copyrights of Images 209

Introduction

A World of Stereotypes, Archetypes, Prototypes, and Other "Types"

The human mind is designed to compartmentalize. That's how it evolved—to see patterns, to seek meaning, even when there is none. It clumps people, situations, foods, and ideas into groups so they can be easily catalogued, stored, and recalled. And for the most part, this works quite well... with some extremely important caveats.

In recent decades, a new field in psychology—behavioral economics—has examined this process in detail. Its two founders, Daniel Kahneman and Amos Tversky, won the Nobel Prize in Economics for demonstrating that the human brain operates with two primary systems of thought.

System 1 is the first one. It is fast, intuitive, impulsive. It jumps to conclusions. It takes shortcuts. It's how we survive a complicated world without overloading our brain. System 2 is the second one. It is slower, more analytical, more deliberate—but it's rarely in the driver's seat.

The reason? System 1 evolved out of necessity. A caveman on the savanna saw a rustling plant. Was it the wind? A rabbit? A lion? If he assumed it wasn't a threat, and he was wrong, he'd be dead. But if he assumed it was a lion—whether or not it was—he'd live to tell the tale. That's heuristics. That's System 1. Jumping to conclusions with limited data, simply because there's no time for careful reasoning.

That same shortcut logic drives our need for stereotypes.

As we built civilization—our tribes, cities, industries, and institutions—we needed a way to quickly size people up. Enter the archetypes of Carl Jung: fundamental human categories that live in our collective unconscious. Over time, these archetypes became stereotypes—more rigid, more exaggerated, more absurd, less useful, and often completely wrong.

Yet every stereotype has some basis in reality. Otherwise, it wouldn't exist. But like System 1, stereotypes reduce the infinite complexity of human personality to a cartoon. They flatten everything into a Three Stooges routine of lazy assumptions, with none of the originality or craft that made Larry, Curly, and Moe actual geniuses of their art.

Stereotypes are seductive. They offer quick, comfortable answers. You see a man with a cowboy hat, a drawl, and a pistol on his belt—you assume he's from Texas, votes Republican, and lives on a ranch. But you could be wrong. Maybe he's a billionaire from Manhattan who just likes dressing Western, imitating accents and loves guns. Or you might see a man in a suit stepping out of a limousine—you assume he's a wealthy executive. Maybe he's a rancher who just left a board meeting... or a swindler trying to get you to believe he is successful.

You don't know. But your brain thinks you do. And that's the problem.

This book is about the people who break that logic. The stereotype busters. The misfits who don't fit.

Some look the part but don't live it. Others live the part but don't look it. Some look and live it—and then defy it anyway.

That's why I wrote this book. To gather in one place the stories of nearly fifty people—from every walk of life, every era, and every discipline—who smashed the boxes that the world tried to put them in. It's a kind of island of misfit toys. You'll meet some of the most famous people in the world. Some of the most important. And some you've never heard of—but never will forget.

Here you'll meet:

1. A man who had the chance to be king and emperor for life—and said no.
2. A military drill sergeant who became the world's gentlest painter.
3. A super-bust pornstar who never had sex on camera and was also a Citibank finance officer.
4. A libertarian President who hated government—and lived by it.
5. A tech mogul from Arkansas who dressed like a mechanic.
6. A far-right conservative who was pro-choice, pro-gay, pro-black, pro-abortion, and pro-everything.

You'll meet a porn star who is also a philosopher and Zen practitioner, a film critic duo who made movies accessible for everyone, a magician who used tricks to promote science, a rich man who lived like a monk, a rock star who never touched drugs, a mountain man who was a deep philosopher, a Jewish Professional wrestler who looks like an outlaw biker, and a Southern football linebacker with a PhD in psychology.

You'll meet an 80s actor star who's also a Shakespearean professor fluent in Ancient Greek and Latin, a cowboy who was a socialist, a general who refused to scream, a world leader who rejected power, a peace activist who defeated the world's largest empire without raising a single weapon, a man who created the most advanced libertarian government ever without ever so much as attending a single day of school, a former president whose greatest achievements happened after leaving office, a meatpacking plant security guard who changed an entire sport with sheer mathematics, and much, much, more

This is not fiction. These people lived. They made history. They changed everything. And they didn't do it by fitting in. They did it by breaking the mold.

This book is for everyone who's ever looked at someone and made a snap judgment. And it's for everyone who's ever been on the receiving end of one. Because the truth is, you can't assume anything about anyone. Not their strength, not their weakness, not their genius, not their heart.

This is a book of exceptions. Of contradictions. Of people who are greater than the sum of the boxes we put them in.

And in reading about them, I hope you'll see that the world is bigger, wilder, and far more surprising than the stories we tell ourselves about it.

Thanks for reading.

—Dr. Robbie King
Kissimmee, Florida

Chapter 1

Bill Murray
The Fame-Despising Superstar

The Stereotype

Celebrities love fame. They live for it. They want the spotlight, the camera flashes, the adoring fans. And if they pretend to hate the attention, it's often just another way to get more of it. Fame is the ultimate drug—and Hollywood is built on people addicted to it.

The Reality

Enter Bill Murray (1950-Present). One of the most successful, highest-paid actors of the 1980s—who walked away from it all at the height of his fame. A man who didn't just dislike fame—he despised it. So much so that he disappeared from Hollywood, fled to France, and spent years studying poetry and eating candy in silence, while the world begged him to come back.

The Obliteration of a Stereotype

Hollywood runs on dreams: The dream of being discovered, of walking red carpets, of paparazzi, awards shows, mansions, and billion-dollar franchises. Thousands of hopeful people move to Los Angeles every year chasing that dream. They wait tables, go to auditions, and fantasize about being the next superstar. And the public assumes all actors—especially successful ones—want that. That they need the fame like an addict needs their fix.

But like every stereotype, that one is based on exaggeration. And Bill Murray is the exception that blows it to pieces.

Born in 1950 in Winnetka, Illinois, Murray grew up in a large Irish Catholic family and he was a non-conformist from the beginning. His father died when he was 17, which changed the course of his life. He got into fights. He had run-ins with the law. He played amateur baseball but fell asleep on the field, mid-game. He had a wild streak... in fact, he was a wild streak—and always lived life on his own terms.

He broke out on *Saturday Night Live* in the 70s and then went on to star in many noteworthy movies, most importantly *Meatballs*, *Caddyshack*, and of course, *Ghostbusters*, where he played Peter Venkman in the second-highest grossing movie of 1984 and a true cultural juggernaut. As a result of that last picture, Murray-mania swept the country. He was offered everything: starring roles, cameos, millions of dollars and was constantly pursued by everyone he saw for a coveted autograph. He could have been the face of the 80s (as big as or even bigger than Sylvester Stallone, Chevy Chase, or even Arnold Schwarzenegger). He was on his way to being the highest-paid, most omnipresent actor in the business.

But at the height of his fame—he said no.

He didn't want to become a brand. He didn't want to be *that* guy. He didn't want to be approached. He didn't want to be adored. He didn't want to live life on someone else's terms.

So, he vanished.

He moved to Paris soon after the release of *Ghostbusters*. He studied French poetry at the Sorbonne University. He watched vintage cinema. He ate artisanal candy. He lived privately, deliberately, and off the grid. He turned down multi-million-dollar roles on multiple occasions. He refused to play the game. Instead of hiring an agent, he set up a 1-800 number where producers could leave messages—and then he might check them.

He reemerged only when he was ready—with a small role in *Little Shop of Horrors* a few years later, and then later, with the 1993 masterpiece *Groundhog Day*. One of the most perfectly crafted films of its era. And he still hated how popular he had become and still hid from the limelight.

Murray's life became the stuff of legend. He was known to crash weddings, steal fries from strangers' plates, sign autographs incorrectly on purpose, or disappear from sets for hours without prediction or explanation. Not out of arrogance—but out of sheer disinterest in the fake rituals of stardom.

He loved baseball. He loved his mother. He was known for being brutally honest and radically unpredictable. He could be incredibly kind—or sharply dismissive. It depended on how you approached him. And he refused to live anywhere near Hollywood.

He still doesn't have a manager. Or a publicist. Or a fixed address. Or a cell phone. He accepts roles when he feels like it. He does interviews only when he's in the mood. He acts only on projects that resonate with him, and works with directors he respects—on his own time, in his own way.

And while he did make tens of millions and starred in many classics—*Ghostbusters, Scrooged, What About Bob?, Rushmore, Lost in Translation, The Life Aquatic, The Royal Tenenbaums* and many more—he never played the fame game.

He broke the mold completely.

In a world where everyone wants to be famous, and where the famous want to be worshipped, Bill Murray quietly chose to disappear. And somehow, by disappearing, he became even more legendary.

He never needed the spotlight to shine.
He never needed the machine to matter.
He never needed to be liked—only to be real.

He didn't just walk away from fame—he outlived it.
And that's as stereotype-breaking as it gets.

That's Bill Murray.

Chapter 2

F.W. De Klerk
The Dictator Who Dismantled his Own Regime

F.W. De Klerk shaking Nelson Mandela's hand. They both shared the Nobel Peace Prize for the peaceful end of Apartheid South Africa and transition to democracy.

The Stereotype

Dictators love power. They consolidate it, hoard it, and use it to crush opposition. Power corrupts, and absolute power corrupts absolutely. From Stalin to Mao, from Hitler to Mussolini, from Caesar to Kim Jong-un—history is filled with tyrants who never let go.

The Reality

Enter F.W. de Klerk (1936-2021). The only dictator in history who voluntarily and systematically dismantled the oppressive regime he ruled. A man who, out of conscience, chose to end his own power and return it to the people.

The Obliteration of a Stereotype

In the United States, African history is often overlooked—a footnote, a rounding error, a distant echo in world affairs. But the history of Africa, and specifically, in this case, South Africa is not just important—it is vital to understanding the arc of power, race, and redemption in the 20th century.

Following a long period of British colonization, brutality, and displacement, South Africa formalized one of the most destructive systems of racial segregation in history: apartheid. Officially implemented in 1948, apartheid divided the nation into rigid racial classes, structuring society in the following way:

1. **White Boers** (Afrikaners – Dutch-descended white Africans) at the very top, in total political control.
2. **Non-Boer whites** (British, Portuguese, Greek, Jewish and other minorities) at a close second, holding full citizenship and allowed to run businesses, but not for political office.
3. **Mixed-race individuals** (known as Coloureds, -distinct from the similar Jim Crow terminology in the U.S.- which themselves were stratified by their cultural and racial proximity to Boers, with Boer Coloureds at the top, followed by other "mixes").
4. **Descendants of immigrants from the Indian Subcontinent.**
5. **Black Africans,** at the bottom, with no civil rights or even citizenship.

It was a horrible caste system of control, built on racial classification and legalized inequality.

South Africa's government was run entirely by white elites, with its police force militarized and brutal, and its elections a fiction. Dissent was punished with death, hard labor, lengthy automatic prison sentences and summary executions as well as police and army massacres. Civil rights were nonexistent. Its riches—diamonds, gold, minerals—flowed upward, creating luxury for a few and suffering for millions.

Other nations sanctioned South Africa severely and condemned it extensively, but its rulers dug in and doubled down on the system. They created nuclear weapons, expanded the military, and tightened their grip, committing massacres on peaceful civilians and much worse. Every ruler prior to F.W. de Klerk entrenched the system further. And then, in the late 1980s, something unprecedented happened.

De Klerk, an Afrikaner born into the elite ruling class, assumed the presidency. By all appearances, he was just another in a long line of white rulers. But within him was something different: a sense of ethics that defied the machinery of power.

He realized that the system was not only economically unsustainable—but morally bankrupt.

He could have done what so many others had done. He could have leaned on the military. He could have used South Africa's nuclear arsenal as leverage. He could have jailed more dissidents, crushed more uprisings, and painted himself as the savior of Afrikaner rule.

But he didn't.

Instead, F.W. de Klerk did what no one expected: He released Nelson Mandela, who had campaigned against apartheid and for equal rights to all, from prison with a full pardon.

He entered into years of negotiations. He granted full voting rights and constitutional equality to all South Africans. He opened the door to the nation's first free elections. He peacefully transitioned power to the very people his regime had once oppressed.

And perhaps most astonishingly—he voluntarily dismantled South Africa's nuclear weapons and turned them over to the United Nations (the first and only country to ever do it).

He did not lose power. He gave it away. He did not ask for forgiveness. He offered it first.

He stood before the world and issued a full, formal apology—not a half-measure, not a statement of regret, but a sweeping, comprehensive acknowledgment of the injustice and suffering apartheid had caused.

No other colonial power—not Britain, not Spain, not France, not Portugal, not Belgium, not Russia—has ever issued such an apology. None of them dismantled their empires voluntarily. None of them offered reparations in the form of democratic control and full citizenship. But F.W. de Klerk did.

And he paid a price. He was reviled by many within his own community. He was branded a traitor by Afrikaner hardliners. He could have ruled for decades—he chose, instead, to walk away.

South Africa today is not perfect. Its challenges are immense. But it is free. Its citizens vote. Its laws, while flawed, are no longer built on skin color. And it all began with a decision that no dictator before or since has made.

Nelson Mandela may have been the moral heart of the revolution. But without de Klerk, there would have been no revolution at all. And he won the Nobel Peace Prize (sharing it with Mandela) for it.

In a world of dictators who build prisons, F.W. de Klerk built a door. And then—he stepped aside, and let others walk through it.

That's F.W. de Klerk.

Chapter 3

Tom Selleck

The Super Relaxed Suntanned Smoothie Who Was Actually the Hardest Worker in Hollywood

The Stereotype

Tall, slim, muscular, good-looking playboys with deep tans who live on the beach, drive Ferraris, reside in mansions, and coast through life in the fast lane despise hard work, and live only for pleasure.

The Reality

Enter Tom Selleck (1945-Present). One of the most down-to-earth, methodical, perseverance-driven, Protestant work ethic champions of our time. The king of steady grit. The anti-playboy.

The Obliteration of a Stereotype

For those old enough to remember the primetime tv series *Magnum P.I.*—and yes, Selleck himself has pointed out how odd it is that it had "P.I." in the title—the show gave us Thomas Magnum: the archetype of the American male fantasy in the early '80s. Magnum lived on Oahu, Hawaii, in a sprawling beachfront mansion. He drove a cherry-red Ferrari. He took on cases only when he felt like it, lived by his own rules, hung out with his buddies, surfed, swam, and dated the most stunning women on the planet. He had the perfect tan, the perfect mustache, and the perfect carefree life.

The show didn't invent the stereotype—it solidified it. It carried on a tradition going back to the dawn of the Playboy ideal. Hugh Hefner codified it in the '50s. JFK embodied it. James Bond glamorized it. Magnum lived it. And Tom Selleck looked like the very soul of that myth.

But he wasn't.

That's what makes him belong in this book.

Because the very purpose of this project is to remind us that just because someone looks like something, doesn't mean they are that thing.

Tom Selleck is not a suntanned smoothie. He is not a slacker playboy. He is everything but that.

Born to a humble California family—his father an airplane mechanic, his mother a homemaker—Selleck grew up without wealth or privilege. He's recounted how, as a kid, he wrecked a car and feared not just the punishment, but how his parents could possibly afford to cover the damages.

Discipline wasn't just present in his home—it was carved into him. And Selleck made it his code. He became a true disciple of the Protestant work ethic: delaying gratification, embracing consistency, grinding forward while others coasted on talent.

Selleck has a personal phrase: "It's time to lay bricks." When life gets out of hand, when he needs grounding, he returns to work—literally. He grabs bricks and builds.

He walked on to the USC basketball team and made it to the starting roster (an incredibly difficult feat), worked his way to a scholarship, started modeling, then moved into commercials—gradually, patiently. He leveraged his looks, but never coasted on them. He studied acting from scratch, worked his way up, and finally broke through.

When *Magnum P.I.* ended, in fact, Selleck gave his bonus paycheck for the final season to the crew—those who helped build the show. No fanfare. No publicity stunt. Just quiet generosity.

Today, he spends his time on his ranch. He trims his own bushes. He builds his own sheds. He doesn't have a cell phone and he doesn't use email. Not out of vanity or performative humility, but because he simply doesn't want to be distracted. He lives life on his terms—not for the spotlight.

And unlike the playboys whose images often cracked under pressure Selleck stayed clean. One quiet divorce. One long, happy marriage. No arrests. No headlines. No mess.

Drafted into Vietnam, he served in the California National Guard. His unit was prepared for combat deployment and he was ready for it—but President Johnson's last-minute decision kept them home. Selleck stayed in for five years. Rose to sergeant. Never bragged about it.

Everything about him looks like the archetype of the effortless man of leisure. But in truth, he is more like an American lumberjack in disguise—with a mustache.

In the end, Tom Selleck may have played the ultimate suntanned smoothie. But in real life, he laid bricks.

That's Tom Selleck.

Chapter 4

Dr. Hugo Eckener
The Tycoon Who Dismantled His Empire for the Sake of Ethics

Dr. Hugo Eckener (fourth from left) with President Calvin Coolidge at the White House, 1924.

The Stereotype

Businessmen are only in it for profit. Ethics don't matter. When money's on the line, they'll do anything. Cut corners. Lie. Sell out. Make deals with devils. History is full of corporate leaders who sided with tyrants, turned a blind eye, and chose riches over righteousness.

The Reality

Enter Dr. Hugo Eckener (1868-1954), Psychologist, Engineer, Pilot, Aventurer, Entrepreneur. The only man to ever make airships (blimps, though they are technically different) massively profitable. A pioneer. A dreamer. A tycoon. And when it mattered most—a man of unbreakable conscience who chose principle over power, and in doing so, destroyed his own empire to avoid enabling a genocidal regime.

The Obliteration of a Stereotype

Once upon a time, about a hundred years ago, airplanes and airships were locked in a race to conquer the skies. And for a while, airships were winning.

They carried more passengers. They had more range. They were smoother, quieter, and more luxurious. They completed the first true transatlantic flights—not short hops from Newfoundland to Ireland, but full crossings. They flew the first paying passengers, the first round-the-world flights, the first cross-Pacific routes and the first paying cargo. For a golden moment, they were the future.

At the center of it all stood one man: Dr. Hugo Eckener.

Though the modern airship was invented by his mentor, Count Ferdinand von Zeppelin, it was Eckener who perfected it. He captained the Graf Zeppelin (the most successful airship ever, with 10 years of continuous service) on its legendary flights and was instrumental in developing over 100 different blimps. He turned airships into a profitable, respected, and sustainable form of international travel. He was, in every sense, the Steve Jobs of the sky.

And then the Nazis took over.

Like many German (and non-German companies operating in Germany at the time)—BMW, Siemens, Coca Cola, Hugo Boss, and others—the Zeppelin company came under pressure to serve the Reich. But Dr. Eckener was not a Nazi. In fact, he despised them. He made it known publicly. He refused to join the party. He refused to praise Hitler. He even resisted flying the Nazi flag—agreeing only to place it on one end of the ship, and deliberately maneuvering his airships to keep it out of view during landings and flybys.

But there was a bigger problem: hydrogen.

Airships floated because they were filled with hydrogen, a buoyant but highly flammable gas. And the Hindenburg, the pride of Eckener's fleet, was designed to run on helium—a safe, non-flammable alternative. But there was only one country in the world that had it in large supply: the United States.

Unfortunately, America had placed a ban on exporting helium, especially to Germany, fearing the gas might be used for military purposes. The order was signed by President Franklin D. Roosevelt and was deemed irrevocable.

So, Eckener made the boldest move of his career. He flew to the United States to meet with FDR personally. He told him: I want to move my company here. I want to build the airships in America, fill them with helium, and escape the grip of the Nazi regime.

FDR listened. He respected Eckener's courage. He told him: *"I can't start a U.S. airship program again. The crashes of the Macon, Akron, and Shenandoah* (the three biggest American airships) *have ended that possibility. But I can give you the helium. Quietly. You can bring the Hindenburg here, deflate its hydrogen, fill it with helium in Kansas, and return to Germany safely. I'll allow that—for you, and you alone."*

Dr. Eckener had every reason to say yes. He had a business empire to save. Thousands of jobs. Decades of work. World fame. Personal fortune.

But he said no.

He looked the President of the United States in the eye and told him:

"Mr. President, I cannot take your offer. Because I cannot guarantee the Nazis won't seize my company, imprison me or send me to a concentration camp, and use those helium-filled airships to bomb you, your allies, or any other innocent people. I will not let my life's work become a tool of evil."

He returned to Germany empty-handed.

And just as he feared—it happened.

The Nazi regime stripped him of his position. Hermann Göring (Nazi war criminal and head of the Nazi air force) removed him from command. The Zeppelin company continued without him. His crowning achievement, the Hindenburg, flew without him at the helm—and he wasn't there to warn the crew about the danger of static electricity, aggressive turns, and the idle hovering around thunderstorms. He wasn't there to stop the disaster.

The Graf Zeppelin II, designed as the most advanced airship in the world (a more advanced twin of the Hindenburg), was never used for passengers. Without helium, it was relegated to surveillance, propaganda flights, and eventually scrapped for metal. The dream of passenger airships died.

After the war, Eckener tried to restart the Zeppelin program. But the world had moved on. Airplanes had taken over. The Nazi stain on airships lingered. The world had no appetite for their return.

Eckener, once the most respected airship commander in the world, died forgotten. His company dismantled. His life's work gone.

But what he didn't lose—was his soul.

While countless German companies cozied up to the Nazis and made fortunes off genocide, Eckener made a different choice. He chose conscience over convenience. Silence over complicity. And integrity over everything.

We're told businessmen are greedy. Ruthless. Unethical. Willing to make deals with tyrants if it lines their pockets.

But Hugo Eckener reminds us: Sometimes, rarely, the tycoon does the right thing. Even when it costs him everything.

That's Dr. Hugo Eckener.

Chapter 5

Ross Perot
The Redneck Tech Genius Who Tried to Save the Republic

Ross Perot (left), during the 1992 presidential debate alongside George H. W. Bush and Bill Clinton.

The Stereotype

Rednecks are dumb. A thick Southern drawl means you're uneducated. A rural background means you can't understand policy. If you're from the American heartland you're expected to know about tractors, cattle, and football, not economics, global strategy, or federal reform.

The Reality

Enter Ross Perot (1930-2019). The self-made billionaire from Texarkana, right on the Texas-Arkansas border. A tech magnate before Silicon Valley had a name. A man who stood on national TV in a $50 suit, with flip charts, and calmly explained how to balance the federal budget, fix the economy and the country completely. A man who nearly became president... twice—and who, even in defeat, changed American politics forever.

The Obliteration of a Stereotype

In today's politically fractured landscape, few groups are more casually mocked than the rural, Southern, working-class man. The drawl. The boots. The manners. It's all treated as a punchline. The assumption is always the same: if you sound like a redneck, you must be dumb.

But stereotypes don't survive facts. And Ross Perot was a walking, talking statistical outlier.

Perot had every surface-level quality the stereotype demands, including the thick Texas accent, the Cowboy straight-talk and the rural roots.

But that's where the stereotype stopped cold.

Ross Perot was a genius. He was a visionary entrepreneur, a data-driven reformer, a systems thinker, and a policy radical who spent decades studying how to rebuild the U.S. government from the ground up.

Before Elon Musk. Before Steve Jobs. Before Peter Thiel... There was Ross Perot.

He built Electronic Data Systems (EDS) from nothing into a multibillion-dollar tech services empire.

He was a tech mogul in the 1960s and 70s—in Texas—before it was cool.

But that wasn't the peak of his life.

The peak was when he decided to run for President of the United States, not as a Republican, not as a Democrat—but as an independent. And he didn't just try. He dominated the early polls.

At one point in the 1992 election, Ross Perot was leading the race for President. An independent candidate… From Texas… With no party machinery. Just a vision, a brain, and the guts to tell the truth.

And what did he do?

He bought airtime on national television (from his own pocket)—entire hours—and walked the American people through the federal debt crisis as well as a thorough plan to rebuild the economy and the country using charts, graphs, and math. No slogans. No bumper stickers. Just facts. Clear, direct, honest facts.

He had a full plan to:

1. Balance the federal budget
2. Eliminate the deficit and the debt
3. Shrink the size of government
4. Cut unnecessary bureaucracy
5. Create a fully functional, efficient and affordable Universal Healthcare System
6. Reform taxes
7. Bring fiscal sanity back to the United States
8. End unnecessary wars
9. Prioritize working-class Americans
10. Rebuild the country's infrastructure.
11. And revive the economy through sheer accountability and logic

And it wasn't theoretical. It was practical. Detailed. Operational.

He didn't offer soundbites. He offered solutions. And the public? They listened. He won nearly 20% of the popular vote—an unprecedented achievement in modern third-party history. He changed the entire race, splitting the vote and paving the way for Bill Clinton's victory. And in doing so, he rewrote what was possible in American politics.

Yes, he dropped out temporarily—after rumors of political operatives threatening his family—and it damaged his chances. But he came back and still dominated the debates.
Yes, he was mocked for his voice, his ears, his delivery and even his height.

But no one could deny the reality. Ross Perot knew more about how to fix the government than anyone else in the race.
And he cared more about the country than his own ego.

He wasn't in it for power. He was in it for the repair of the republic.

Ross Perot shattered every notion of what a Southern man could be. He wasn't just a rich redneck. He wasn't just a data nerd in cowboy boots. He was a man who almost changed the direction of the entire nation—and had a plan ready to go on Day One.

His legacy? It remains alive and well to this day:

1. The debt conversation in American politics began with him.
2. The rise of outsider candidates began with him.
3. The idea that you don't have to speak like a Harvard professor to be smarter than one? Ross Perot proved it.

He spoke with a twang.
He wore Texas suits.
He told the truth like it was a bullet.

And he nearly became President of the United States twice doing it.

He didn't fit the mold.
He melted it down, recast it, and hung it from a nail in his barn.

Ross Perot wasn't just a stereotype breaker.
He was a walking, talking case study in why stereotypes fail.

That's Ross Perot.

Chapter 6

Barry Goldwater

The Pro-Choice, Pro-Civil Rights, Pro-Minorities, Pro-Labor, Pro-Feminism, Anti-Racist, Pro-LGBTQ+, Pro-Drug, Anti-Religious Fervor, Far-Right Conservative

The Stereotype

Conservatives are pro-life. They're anti-gay, anti-drug, anti-civil rights, anti-minority. They love religion, hate feminism, fear change, and reject all forms of social progress. Conservatives cling to the past and block the future. In today's politics, to be conservative is to be the opposite of liberal in every way imaginable.

The Reality

Enter Barry Goldwater (1909-1998). Arizona cowboy. 1964 Republican presidential nominee. Author of *The Conscience of a Conservative*. One of the most economically conservative minds in American history—and also one of the most socially liberal. A man who didn't just challenge the political spectrum. He blew it up.

The Obliteration of a Stereotype

Today's political landscape forces everything into binaries. You're left or right. Blue or red. Conservative or liberal. But real politics—real philosophy—isn't one-dimensional. It's not a straight line. It's a grid, a compass and a quadrant. And Barry Goldwater lived in the uncharted space between those poles, where most people are too afraid to stand.

Born in 1909, in the still-wild Arizona Territory, Goldwater grew up in the final flickers of the Old West. Wyatt Earp was still alive and well. Arizona wasn't even a state yet.

Goldwater didn't grow up in Washington. He grew up with ranchers, miners, traders, and fiercely independent people who didn't wait for the government to tell them how to live. His worldview was forged in that furnace of personal freedom.

And yes—Barry Goldwater was a conservative. A true economic conservative. He believed in small government, fiscal discipline, individual responsibility. He believed in capitalism without a safety net, and he made no apologies for it.

But when it came to personal freedom—he was as liberal as it gets.

1. He was pro-choice (famously even taking his own daughter to get an abortion).
2. He was pro-LGBTQ+, long before it was politically safe, even pushing to allow them entry into the armed forces decades before actual integration.
3. He was pro-drug decriminalization.
4. He was pro-civil rights—and deeply respected by Black leaders for his constitutional defense of freedom, even if he disagreed with federal overreach.
5. He was pro-minorities, spending his entire life working for the rights of native Americans and being one of the few employers to consistently hire African Americans and Mexican Americans during the segregation era.
6. He was anti-religious interference in government and warned evangelicals to stay out of politics (even insulting them when they pushed in too much).
7. He was pro-woman, pro-individual, pro-dignity in every sense.

This wasn't theoretical. He lived it. He operated his department store empire with it. He legislated it. He ran for president on it. He wrote the definitive book on it.

Goldwater believed government had no right to tell people how to live their private lives—any people. That meant no bans on abortion, no bans on drugs, no bans on marriage. The government's job, in his mind, was to stay out of both your pocket and your bedroom.

And he wasn't quiet about it. When President Nixon was cornered during the Watergate scandal, it was Barry Goldwater who told him to resign... and Goldwater was the only person Nixon listened to.

When religious conservatives began to hijack the Republican Party, Goldwater pushed back, famously saying:

"Every good Christian should kick Jerry Falwell (a Baptist minister and conservative activist) *in the ass."*

That was Barry Goldwater. No filter. No apologies. Just a man who lived and breathed personal liberty—and wasn't afraid to be hated for it.

He was demonized during his campaign for president in 1964—portrayed as a warmonger, mocked as a trigger-happy lunatic… and he lost in a landslide.

But time has re-evaluated Barry Goldwater. Because for all his hawkishness, he never started a war. For all his economic strictness, he never sold out. And for all his conservative branding, he was more socially progressive than most modern liberals.

He was a senator, a thinker, a firebrand, and a rebel—in a cowboy hat and shotgun in hand.

He didn't play to party lines. He drew his own map.

He broke the biggest stereotype in politics: **That you can't be a fiscal conservative and a social liberal at the same time. That "left" and "right" are mutually exclusive.**

Barry Goldwater was both. And neither. And more.

He proved you don't have to choose between freedom of the wallet and freedom of the self.

He showed the world that political nuance isn't weakness—it's strength.

Most people are swallowed by the stereotypes. Barry Goldwater obliterated them.

That's Barry Goldwater.

Chapter 7

Paul Kruger

The Politician Who Despised Government

The Stereotype

Politicians and rulers love big government. They crave power, authority, and control. They want to regulate every aspect of their citizens' lives—from taxes to property, from speech to commerce. They claim it's for the people's good, but they rarely stop expanding their reach.

The Reality

Enter Paul Kruger (1825-1904). The statesman who designed one of the freest, most anti-government governments in history. A man who saw the state not as a source of freedom—but as a threat to it.

The Obliteration of a Stereotype

It's almost impossible today to imagine a system of government so minimal that it barely exists. We live in a world of zoning laws, licensing boards, labor regulations, mandates, subsidies, and red tape. Whether you're trying to hire someone, fire someone, rent out your home, or sell a product, the government is there to tell you how, when, whether you're even allowed to do it and how much money you are to give back to them when you do sell it.

And yet—there was a place where that wasn't true. A place where government didn't just choose to stay out of your life—it was designed to be too weak to interfere in the first place. A place where private property was absolute (no eminent domain nor anything like it). Where disputes were settled privately. Where citizen militias, not standing armies, defended the land. Where taxation and regulation were almost nonexistent. This was the world of the Boer Republics—and their guiding visionary was Paul Kruger.

The Orange Free State, the Natalia Republic, The Republic of Stellaland, the Transvaal: these were four of several fully recognized countries in Southern Africa during the 19th century that were truly libertarian. But unlike other Libertarian examples, they were that not by coincidence. They were libertarian by design. And that design came from Kruger—a man with no formal education, who had read only one book in his entire life: the Bible.

Paul Kruger was born in South Africa and lived through one of its most formative events: the Great Trek. The Boers (Dutch-descended settlers) fled British rule in search of a land where they could live by their own code. Kruger, like many of them, didn't seek power. He sought distance—from control, from coercion, from tyranny.

After settling on his farm, Kruger and a group of compatriots shaped the governmental framework for the Transvaal Republic and in turn, of all the other Boer settlements which later became countries of their own. His vision wasn't "small government." It was almost no government. He didn't want a limited state—he wanted a powerless one. The ideal? A government so weak it couldn't possibly interfere.

No army—just private citizen militias.
No taxes—only voluntary contributions.
No courts—just private arbitration.
No public services—only community action.
No centralized coercion.
And most importantly—absolute property rights.

In America, we often talk about limited government. But from the moment of the Whiskey Rebellion under George Washington, that idea began to erode. Even in the frontier West, libertarianism was more the result of distance than design. The Boer Republics were different. They were intentional. And Kruger, though unlettered in the classical sense, was an ideological architect. He didn't just tolerate minimal government—he believed in it. Fervently. Spiritually.

When the British came to crush the Boers, Kruger and his countrymen—armed farmers, expert marksmen, and fiercely independent citizens—defeated the greatest empire on Earth in the First Anglo-Boer War. And though they lost the second (due to extreme human rights abuses on the part of the British), they earned global respect for their resistance, even receiving military assistance from Russia, Ireland, Germany, and even the United States.

Kruger could have built power for himself. He could have centralized the state. But he didn't. He stayed true to his belief: that freedom matters more than order, and that governments are inherently dangerous when given the power to do good—because they'll eventually use that power to do harm.

Whether Kruger was right or wrong is not the question of this chapter. The fact is: he broke the mold.

Today, even in America's most "free" states—Alaska, Texas, Wyoming, Montana—government overreach still exists. Eminent domain still threatens property. Licensing laws still restrict opportunity. COVID-19 revealed just how far the state can reach, even in places known for rugged individualism.

Had the Boer Republics still existed in 2020, the pandemic would have been irrelevant in policy terms. There would have been no lockdowns. No mandates. No closures. Because the government would have had no power to impose them.

The land was vast. The people lived on 20,000-acre farms—larger than Manhattan. Social distancing wasn't a mandate—it was a lifestyle.

In the end, Kruger—a small man, uneducated by formal standards, who read only the Bible—crafted one of the most radical, freedom-forward systems of government the world has ever seen.

He wasn't a politician who wanted power.
He was a politician who wanted less of it—for everyone.
He didn't build a government.
He built a non-government.
And in doing so, he became perhaps the only ruler in history who fought not to lead his people, but to leave them alone.

That's Paul Kruger.

Chapter 8

Bill Goldberg

The Jewish Man Who Looks Like a Harley-Davidson Biker—and Fights Better Than One, Too

The Stereotype

Jewish men aren't athletic. They're not tough. They're not muscular. They don't fight. They're intellectuals, comedians, financiers, professors—not linebackers. Not bouncers. Not warriors. Not men who look like they were carved out of rock behind a motorcycle bar in Amarillo. The stereotype says Jewish guys don't intimidate anyone. They wear glasses and suits. They don't bench press trucks.

The Reality

Enter Bill Goldberg (1966-Present). NFL player. World Wrestling Entertainment superstar. 6'4", 300-pound slab of steel. A walking wall of American muscle who looks like the offspring of a biker gang, a Marine drill instructor, and a world-champion powerlifter—who also happens to be unapologetically Jewish.

The Obliteration of a Stereotype

For reasons rooted in history, culture, and ignorance, there's a persistent, insidious stereotype that Jewish people—particularly Jewish men—are somehow less physically capable than non-Jewish men. Maybe it's because so many Jews have historically gravitated toward intellectual fields. Maybe it's because centuries of oppression forced Jewish communities to survive through culture and craft, not conquest. Maybe it's because Western culture paints the "tough guy" as a Gentile archetype: the cowboy, the soldier, the steel-jawed Protestant.

Whatever the origin, the stereotype exists. And Bill Goldberg smashed it.

He didn't just reject it—he targeted it. He made it his mission to destroy it.

Goldberg didn't change his name to sound more generic. He didn't lean away from his faith or heritage. He leaned in. And then he charged through it like a linebacker hitting a brick wall—and taking the wall down.

Born in Tulsa, Oklahoma—already breaking geographic expectations—Goldberg was raised in a deeply academic, deeply Jewish family. His mother was a classical musician. His father was a physician. And what did Goldberg choose to be?

A bouncer, an NFL lineman, and then—one of the most dominant wrestlers in the world.

In the 1990s, Goldberg burst onto the wrestling scene like a live-action battering ram. His win streaks became legendary. His intensity was unmatched. He didn't talk much—but when he walked into the ring, everyone listened. He looked like a monster, moved like a linebacker, and hit like a freight train.

And he did it under his real name. The unequivocally Jewish last name of "Goldberg".

Not only that—he was vocal about it. He once said:

"I kept the name Goldberg because I wanted Jewish kids to look at me and know they could be badasses too."

He refused to wrestle on Yom Kippur, the holiest day in Judaism—just like Sandy Koufax refused to pitch. He took his faith seriously. He took his image seriously. And he knew exactly what he was doing: showing the world that you could be Jewish and proud and terrifyingly tough all at once.

He wasn't the first great Jewish athlete—Sandy Koufax, Mark Spitz, Lyle Alzado—all made history. But Goldberg brought it to the front lines of pop culture, in an industry driven by myth, archetype, and testosterone.

And he didn't blend in. He stood out. Proudly. Boldly.

Goldberg broke not just the stereotype, but the fear of the stereotype. Most people who try to break stereotypes get broken by them. But he broke through. He owned the ring. He owned the image. And he did it with zero compromise.

There are plenty of Jewish icons in history—Freud, Marx, Spielberg, Kafka, Landsteiner. Intellectuals, revolutionaries, artists, scientists.

But Goldberg is something rarer: A physical symbol. A counter-punch to centuries of narrow imagery.

And he earned it. Not just with strength, but with intent. He didn't just show Jewish kids they could be strong. He showed the world that Jewish strength doesn't need a disguise.

He didn't hide the name. He made sure you heard it as he slammed you into the mat.

Goldberg.

The name itself became the punchline to a stereotype that no longer had teeth.

That's Bill Goldberg.

Chapter 9

Rick Harrison

The Historian, Scholar, Pawnbroker, and Guardian of Knowledge

Rick Harrison speaking at CPAC 2018, beside a rare print of the Declaration of Independence.

The Stereotype

Pawnbrokers are bottom-feeders. They're predatory vultures who lowball the desperate, destroy value, and take pride in scamming people. Ignorant, unethical, and greedy, they're seen as one step below used car salesmen—and several steps below sewage workers. They're the guys who offer you $200 for a $15,000 watch, and then sell it for $10,000 and smile about it. They're exploiters, nothing more.

The Reality

Enter Rick Harrison (1965-Present). The Las Vegas pawnbroker behind the History Channel's *Pawn Stars*. A self-educated scholar. A lover of history, philosophy, and rare artifacts. A man who turned a pawn shop into a cultural institution—and did it with fairness, curiosity, and intellect. Rick Harrison didn't just break the mold of the sleazy pawnbroker—he bulldozed it, rebuilt it, and turned it into a university disguised as a storefront.

The Obliteration a Stereotype

Pawnbrokers have never had a good reputation. Historically, they've been among the most distrusted figures in society—and for good reason. Many have been shady. Many have taken advantage of the poor and the desperate. The stereotype exists because there's truth behind it.

But Rick Harrison is not that stereotype.

While his business is technically a pawn shop, what he runs is far more akin to a museum—or a live-action lecture hall. The Gold & Silver Pawn Shop in Las Vegas is a place where everyday people walk in with artifacts, antiques, and oddities, and leave not just with money—but with knowledge.

That's what Rick brings: a passion for learning, for history, for stories, for truth.

Yes, the show is polished. Yes, some of the walk-ins are staged. But the knowledge? The deals? The historical breakdowns? That's real. If you've ever watched Rick Harrison talk about an 18th-century flintlock rifle, a Roman coin, or a vintage Beatles record, you'll see a man who lives for the details. He doesn't just buy things—he honors them.

He's not a swindler. He's a broker. He buys fairly, sells fairly, and gives people a real sense of what their items are worth.

Unlike many in his profession, he doesn't lowball every deal. He appraises honestly. Sometimes he offers more than people expect—a lot more. One seller brought in a medal tied to Captain James Cook and asked for $100. Rick told him it was worth far more—and paid accordingly. That's not a scripted act. That's a decision rooted in ethics.

You can visit his shop. You can sell your stuff. You can watch real negotiations happen. And if you've ever seen the inside of Rick Harrison's home in interviews or documentaries, you'll know this isn't just a show. His house is filled with antiques, books, and historical pieces. He lives what he sells. He lives what he loves.

In his memoir, Rick talks about growing up with epilepsy. He spent much of his childhood bedridden—so he read. And read. And read. That early hunger for knowledge stayed with him. It made him. It's the real reason he can speak with intelligence on everything from 17th-century muskets to 1970s sports memorabilia.

He's the polymath pawnbroker. The scholar of the strip mall. The historian behind the glass case.

While the world expected another shady loan shark, Rick gave us something else: a man who adores learning, respects history, and treats people fairly.

He doesn't claim to know everything—but he knows a lot. And what he doesn't know, he finds an expert who does. That's what a real scholar does. He learns. He listens. He shares.

Rick Harrison isn't a sleazeball in a biker vest. He just looks like one. That's the magic of it. That's the misdirection. And that's what makes him a perfect fit for this book.

Because when one of the shadiest professions in history gets redefined by a man who loves knowledge, you know a stereotype has been shattered.

And Rick Harrison did it—with a smile, a handshake, and probably a sarcastic joke about Chumlee.

That's Rick Harrison.

Chapter 10

Albert Schweitzer

The Man Who Mastered Everything

Albert Schweitzer walking outside his hospital in Lambaréné, Gabon, Africa.

The Stereotype

You have to pick one thing. If you want to be great, you must devote your life to a single field. Specialize. Focus. The world belongs to the obsessed. You can't be good at more than one thing—maybe you can dabble, maybe have hobbies—but excellence demands sacrifice. No one becomes world-class at multiple disciplines. That's fantasy.

The Reality

Enter Albert Schweitzer (1875-1965). Physician. Humanitarian. Nobel laureate. Theologian. Organist. Music historian. Explorer. Philosopher. Anti-nuclear activist. Author of dozens of books. A man so staggeringly gifted across so many fields that calling him "multi-talented" feels like an insult.

The Obliteration of a Stereotype

We live in a world obsessed with lanes.

Everyone is told to specialize early, declare a major, stick to a brand. Even polymaths today are usually confined to adjacent fields—comedian-screenwriter, director-producer, author-podcaster. A wide-ranging thinker is a rarity. A world-class expert in more than one unrelated field? Virtually unheard of, even frowned upon.

And then there's Albert Schweitzer.

Born in Alsace—a region caught between France and Germany—he did more with one life than most institutions do with a hundred people.

Let's try to count it.

1. **Physician:** Schweitzer earned his M.D. and became one of the world's leading experts in tropical diseases and practiced medicine for decades.
2. **Hospital Creator and Manager:** He founded and personally operated a large hospital in Gabon for decades, providing care to thousands in one of the most underserved regions of Africa. Not for photo ops—for life.

3. **Humanitarian:** He won the Nobel Peace Prize in 1952 for his philosophy of "Reverence for Life," and for dedicating his career to healing others, often under grueling conditions.
4. **Musician:** Not just a casual pianist. Schweitzer was a world-class organist (one of the hardest instruments to play), capable of performing some of the most difficult pieces in the existence.
5. **Music Historian:** He became the world's leading authority on Johann Sebastian Bach, writing scholarly works still referenced today.
6. **Theologian:** Schweitzer earned a doctorate in theology, wrote one of the most influential books on Jesus Christ— *The Quest of the Historical Jesus*—and was a major figure in liberal Protestantism.
7. **Author:** He wrote dozens of books—on theology, philosophy, medicine, ethics, music, and culture.
8. **Adventurer & Explorer:** He traveled through remote parts of Africa, not for entertainment, but for service.
9. **Activist:** Near the end of his life, Schweitzer became the first major global figure to campaign against nuclear weapons, warning of their existential danger at the dawn of the Cold War.

That's not a résumé. That's a civilizational inventory.

In each of these fields, Schweitzer didn't just participate—he excelled. He didn't dabble in music—he defined an era of musicology. He didn't volunteer—he built a hospital. He didn't write books—he shaped disciplines. He didn't theorize ethics—he lived it.

Albert Schweitzer defied the idea that you had to choose.

He didn't just break the stereotype of specialization— He annihilated it. He put specialization on a stretcher and operated on it himself.

He showed us that excellence is not a zero-sum game. That mastery is not finite. That if you are disciplined, curious, and moral, you can—with relentless effort—build a life that touches every great corner of human endeavor with world-class level expertise.

And he did it without ego. Without brand. Without marketing. He lived humbly, worked endlessly, and took no pride in anything except service.

We look at da Vinci as the pinnacle of the polymath ideal. But Schweitzer—a modern man with modern demands and limitations—surpassed him... or more accurately, wiped the floor with him.

Da Vinci theorized. Schweitzer did.
Da Vinci sketched helicopters. Schweitzer built hospitals.
Da Vinci painted beauty. Schweitzer healed suffering.

And unlike most people who achieve at such a high level, Schweitzer didn't seek status. He barely spoke of his own accomplishments. He saw it all—every book, every note, every life saved—as a duty.

There's no one like him. There may never be again.

Albert Schweitzer is the answer to every excuse, every doubt, every fear that says:

"I can't. I'm not trained. I'm not qualified. It's not possible."

It is. He proved it.

And in doing so, he became the final word on the limits of human potential.

That's Albert Schweitzer.

Chapter 11

Steve Martin

The Comedian Who Refused to Be One-Dimensional

The Stereotype

Comedians are clowns. They may be funny, but they're shallow. They only know how to joke, deflect, self-destruct. They're damaged, addicted, impulsive. Once the show's over, there's nothing behind the curtain. Comedy is their life—and they can't function outside of it.

The Reality

Enter Steve Martin (1945-Present). Stand-up legend. Screenwriter. Novelist. Playwright. Banjo virtuoso. Magician. Art collector. Art historian. Art scholar. Philosopher. Surrealist. One of the most intelligent, most restrained, most multi-dimensional figures ever to emerge from the world of entertainment.

The Obliteration of a Stereotype

We are living in a comedy age. Stand-up has exploded—hundreds of specials, millions of clips, sold-out arenas, podcast empires. The cultural oxygen is thick with jokes. And yet, the stereotype persists: comedians are tragic savants. Brilliant on stage, broken off it. Often drug-riddled, emotionally unstable, or creatively desperate.

Steve Martin shattered that image like no one else.

In the 1970s and early 80s, Steve Martin wasn't just a comedian—he was the biggest comedian in the world. He sold out stadiums, drew audiences like a rock star, and changed the very DNA of stand-up.

But his act wasn't observational. It wasn't political.

It was surreal, absurd, self-aware, and infused with magic tricks, props, and artifice. It was a performance of performance—and the world couldn't get enough.

Then, at the height of his fame, he walked away.

Why? Because people weren't laughing at the jokes anymore. They were laughing because it was him.

So, he pulled the cord. And never came back. He didn't "retire temporarily." He left stand-up. Forever.

But that was only the beginning of Steve Martin's true career.

He became a screenwriter, crafting films like *L.A. Story*, *The Jerk*, *The Man with Two Brains*, *Roxanne*, and *Bowfinger*— subversive, sophisticated comedies filled with philosophy, irony, and heart.

He became a world-class actor, acting in his own films plus many more by some of the world's most revered directors, including *Planes, Trains and Automobiles* by John Hughes, *Parenthood*, *Father of the Bride*, *Cheaper by the Dozen*, and many more

He wrote novels. And memoirs. And plays. His work has been performed on Broadway, studied in university courses, and praised by literary critics. He moved fluidly between fiction and nonfiction, with intelligence and elegance.

He became a world-class banjo player, touring with musicians decades his junior—and earning Grammys in the process.

Music wasn't a hobby. It was his first love, and he pursued it with discipline and devotion.

He also became an art collector and a scholar of modernism, with one of the most respected private collections in America. He curated exhibitions. He lectured on the aesthetics of Cubism…. And he did it all without scandal, without collapse, and without ego.

Steve Martin breaks the stereotype because he never bought into it.

He wasn't a party guy.
He didn't burn out.
He didn't self-destruct.
He was, in his own words, "just a shy guy from Orange County" who liked books, banjos, and being alone.

He parodied his own industry in *L.A. Story* and *The Jerk*, skewering fame, absurdity, and the entertainment machine—while remaining inside it.

He wasn't just playing the game differently. He changed the game entirely.

Steve Martin is the proof that a comedian can also be a thinker. That the man who makes the world laugh can also make it think. That true depth doesn't require tragedy. And that leaving comedy doesn't mean you were broken—just that you had more to build.

There has never been another Steve Martin. And there probably never will be.

He didn't just step off the stage. He stepped into history—as the man who refused to be a punchline.

That's Steve Martin.

Chapter 12

Peter Weller

The 80s Action Hero with a PhD in Renaissance Studies

The Stereotype

The 1980s action hero is a god of muscle and mayhem. He doesn't think—he acts. He punches before he speaks, speaks only in one-liners, and breaks laws, bones, and enemy militias with equal ease. He's ripped, intense, unstoppable—and intellectually empty. Brains are for sidekicks. Brawn is for legends.

The Reality

Enter Peter Weller (1947-Present)—also known as RoboCop. But in real life? Not a musclehead. Not a one-liner machine. A Classically trained Shakespearean actor. A Renaissance historian. A PhD scholar fluent in classical Latin and ancient Greek, who teaches at Ivy League universities and lectures at the Smithsonian.

The Obliteration of a Stereotype

The 1980s were the golden age of hypermasculinity. Action heroes weren't just characters—they were archetypes.

Think Arnold Schwarzenegger in *Commando*, *Conan*, or *The Terminator*. Sylvester Stallone in *Rambo* or *Rocky*. Dolph Lundgren as Ivan Drago. Steven Seagal snapping necks in *Out for Justice*. Bruce Willis in *Die Hard*, taking out terrorists barefoot. Mel Gibson and Danny Glover in the *Lethal Weapon* franchise, waging a two-man war on crime. Chuck Norris, roundhouse-kicking the Cold War into submission. Clint Eastwood, squinting down the barrel of "Make my day."

These weren't actors—they were mythology.

And in that pantheon, one of the most enduring—and arguably the most conceptually badass—was RoboCop. Half-man, half-machine. All justice. He didn't just shoot accurately—he vaporized gangsters with precision and moral fury. He didn't just survive gunfire—he walked through it like a god with a badge.

And the man inside the suit?

Peter Weller.

He wasn't the most muscular of the action heroes. He wasn't the most physically intimidating.

But he was one of the most compelling. And behind that steel jaw and that iconic RoboCop voice was an academic scholar disguised as a cyborg.

Weller started his career as a classically trained actor—a real Shakespeare guy. But it wasn't just an MFA. He later went back to school and earned:

1. A master's degree in Roman and Renaissance Art History
2. A PhD in Italian Renaissance Studies from UCLA
3. Mastery of classical Latin and ancient Greek
4. Teaching positions at Syracuse University, UCLA, and lectures at the Smithsonian

While other action heroes were hawking protein powder and starring in B-movie sequels, Weller was translating ancient texts and explaining Michelangelo's brushwork to grad students.

Let that sink in:

The man who played RoboCop can also teach you about Petrarch, papal patronage, and the linguistic evolution of Latin declensions.

He didn't just break the mold—he left it behind, sculpted a bust of Erasmus, and taught it at a university symposium.

And it wasn't just that. He also went on to become a respected TV director, working on shows like *Sons of Anarchy*, *Longmire*, and *Hawaii Five-0*. His career isn't a stunt. It's a fusion of grit and intellect, performance and depth.

Peter Weller is the living contradiction of the action hero stereotype.

He wasn't Arnold's bulk. He wasn't Stallone's intensity. He wasn't Seagal's swagger. He was something smarter, quieter, deeper.

He played a cyborg—and then taught the Renaissance. He killed villains on-screen—and then deconstructed 15th-century Venetian frescoes in a lecture hall. He looked like steel—but carried a library in his mind.

So, the next time you watch RoboCop, remember this:

The baddest machine of justice in 80s cinema… was portrayed by a man who can read Virgil in the original Latin.

And in the pantheon of stereotype breakers, Peter Weller doesn't just deserve a place—he wrote the thesis on it.

That's Peter Weller.

Chapter 13

Elvira

The Gothic Valley Girl — Mistress of the Dark, Master of Reinvention

The Stereotype

Gothic Halloween icons are dark, brooding, sinister, maybe even unhinged. They live in shadow and feed off shock. And if they're women, they're femme fatales with edge—but no warmth. They're Vampyra, Morticia, or Wednesday Addams—cool, composed, and cold. No light. No fun. Certainly not a valley girl.

The Reality

Enter Elvira, Mistress of the Dark, the stage name of Cassandra Peterson (1951-Present). The Halloween icon with a valley girl voice, pin-up curves, and relentless wit. The woman behind the teased black wig and plunging neckline? Cassandra Peterson—an entrepreneur, survivor, feminist, sexual abuse survivor, businesswoman, and the definition of resilience in heels.

The Obliteration of a Gothic Stereotype

Elvira didn't just arrive. She inverted everything.

Dressed like a Gothic queen, speaking like a valley girl. Talking about horror movies, while making you laugh out loud. More Marilyn than Morticia. More punk rock satire than dark arts seduction.

She wasn't Vampyra. She wasn't Morticia. She was herself—and that's what made her dangerous.

Cassandra Peterson's career began long before Elvira ever took the stage. Born in rural Kansas, scarred by a childhood accident that left her burned and isolated, she grew into show business through Vegas, Italy, and eventually Los Angeles.

But behind the laugh track was a life of abuse, betrayal, and trauma.

1. She was raped by Wilt Chamberlain, as she later revealed.
2. She was emotionally abused by her mother.
3. She was sexually molested by a neighbor.
4. She survived the AIDS crisis at its worst in San Francisco, losing friends but never her core.
5. She was harassed, rejected, overlooked, and marginalized by Hollywood again and again.

But she kept going. And when no one gave her a lane—she built her own.

Elvira wasn't a fluke. She was a calculated contradiction.

Cassandra Peterson took every stereotype about goth women, horror hosts, and sex symbols—and flipped it by being:
1. Gothic on the outside, but silly, bright, and goofy on the inside.
2. Sexualized on the surface, but entirely in control of her image.
3. Treated like a character, but building a multi-million-dollar brand that she owned.

She starred in her own films (*Elvira: Mistress of the Dark* and its sequel/prequel/sidequel *Elvira's Haunted Hills*), Television Series Pilot, multiple TV Horror Movie Shows as Host, made national ad campaigns (Coors, Pepsi), appeared on *The Tonight Show* at its height, and created a cult empire based on Halloween joy and personal pain turned into power.

Her success wasn't just a costume—it was a statement of the following:

1. That women could use stereotype without becoming it.
2. That a character can be sexy, silly, spooky—and undeniably smart.
3. That resilience isn't about wearing armor—it's about creating it from sequins and sarcasm.

Cassandra Peterson didn't just survive Hollywood. She owned her image. She built her career on contradiction. And she became the single most enduring Halloween figure in American pop culture.

Elvira is proof that stereotypes can be subverted—and then sold back to the world as power… and for a lot of money. She didn't just trick or treat us. She built an empire from the ashes of her trauma, one joke at a time.

She is *the* Gothic valley girl. The woman who wore darkness like a costume—but never let it own her. And she remains, to this day, the Mistress of the Dark—and the Queen of Reinvention.

That's Elvira.

Chapter 14

Nina Hartley

The Pornstar, Philosopher, Nurse, and Feminist Who Obliterated Every Assumption

Nina Hartley addressing the Free Speech Coalition as an educator and activist.

The Stereotype

Porn stars are damaged. They're unintelligent, unstable, drug-ridden, and self-destructive. They're objects, not agents—people without thought, depth, discipline, or voice. They don't contribute to society. They just sell sex until they're discarded. They certainly don't become educators, scholars, or activists. And they absolutely don't outlast the industry.

The Reality

Enter Nina Hartley (1959-Present). Nurse. Author. Philosopher. Sex educator. Activist. Zen practitioner. Feminist. And yes—legendary adult film actress, with a career spanning five decades and counting. She didn't just break the mold. She spoke to it in full paragraphs, cited her sources, outlasted her peers, and wrote a better ending than anyone expected.

The Obliteration of a Stereotype

Born in Berkeley, California, Nina Hartley was raised by deeply intellectual and politically active parents. Her father and mother were blacklisted American communists during McCarthyism. Her mother—a Zen practitioner—instilled in her a lifelong grounding in meditation, philosophy, and spiritual clarity.

Hartley graduated magna cum laude from San Francisco State University, with a Bachelor of Science in Nursing and soon became a registered nurse.

And then—she entered porn.

But unlike many who drift into the industry by circumstance or desperation, Hartley entered with eyes open and agency intact. She made her own choices. She controlled her image. And from her very first film in 1984, she began to forge what would become the longest continuous career in adult entertainment history.

Nina Hartley has appeared in over 1,000 films. She is an AVN Hall of Fame inductee. She became a defining figure in the MILF and Cougar genre before it had a name. And she did it without being chewed up by the system.

But what sets her apart isn't just her longevity. It's her intellect, her discipline, her character, and her activism.

Hartley has written multiple books on sex education, including *Nina Hartley's Guide to Total Sex*. She has produced dozens of educational videos on communication, intimacy, and sexual health. She's lectured at universities, conferences, TEDx events, and even contributed to respected publications like *The Huffington Post, Salon*, and *The New Yorker*.

She is a fierce feminist, but one who breaks from conventional academia. She argues that porn can be empowering, that sex workers deserve respect, and that the dichotomy between "smart women" and "sexual women" is a lie.

She has spoken eloquently on varied and deeply important subjects, such as:

1. The stigma of sex work
2. The misogyny embedded in puritanical culture
3. The need for honest, open sex education
4. The value of sexual autonomy

She's not just participating in porn—she's redefining how we understand it.

And what's even more stereotype-breaking is that Hartley never descended into addiction. She never lost her moral compass. She has remained monogamous, clear-minded, centered, and grounded.

She's also a Zen student, a public intellectual, and a woman who chose her path, stayed on it, and kept climbing—without compromise.

In an industry where most stars are forgotten in months, she's lasted decades. In a culture that degrades sex workers, she demanded respect. In a society that believes porn stars can't think—she wrote essays that left academics stunned.

There are famous names in adult film history: Jenna Jameson, Lisa Ann, Traci Lords, Tera Patrick, Asia Carrera. But none has matched Nina Hartley in breadth, intellect, longevity, and cultural power.

She didn't just survive porn—she turned it into a platform for truth. She didn't just act—she educated. She didn't just break the stereotype— She flipped it over, dissected it, gave a lecture on it, and then walked away smiling.

Nina Hartley is the ultimate stereotype destroyer. Not just in porn. Not just in feminism.
But perhaps in all of modern entertainment.

That's Nina Hartley.

Chapter 15

Cory Everson

The Muscle Stereotype Destroyer — The Woman Who Made Strength Look Beautiful

The Stereotype

Muscles are for men. A woman with muscle is either compensating for masculinity, emotionally unstable, or trying to erase her femininity. She's "too much." Too hard. Too manly. Women can be toned, sure—but to be muscular is to be broken, unfeminine, unfocused, or insecure.

The Reality

Enter Cory Everson (1958-Present). Six-time Miss Olympia (the highest bodybuilding award in the world). The most celebrated female bodybuilder in history. A woman whose physique was undeniably powerful—but whose grace, poise, femininity, and beauty were never compromised. She didn't just redefine the female form—she redrew the entire blueprint.

The Obliteration of a Stereotype

Before Cory Everson, femininity was always defined in opposition to strength. A woman could be sporty, sure—but not too muscular.

She could be athletic—but only if she stayed within the confines of what was culturally accepted: lean, slim, graceful.

Power was male. Muscle was male. Beauty was fragile.

And then Cory Everson walked onto the stage in the golden era of bodybuilding—and ripped that illusion apart with a smile.

Built under the guidance of Joe Weider, the same man who launched Arnold Schwarzenegger's career and created the modern fitness industry, Corey Everson entered the world of competitive bodybuilding and dominated it.

She didn't just win. She reigned. Six Miss Olympia titles. Unbeaten. Undefeated. Unmatched.

And she did it with a physique that was balanced, defined, powerful, and graceful. She was strong—but not brute. Muscular—but never masculine. She proved that strength and sensuality can coexist in a single body, without contradiction.

Cory wasn't just a competitor. She was a symbol. She appeared in fitness magazines, health columns, and films—most notably in *Double Impact* (1991) alongside Jean-Claude Van Damme at his apex, where she played a powerhouse henchwoman with screen presence as sharp as her abs.

She went on to become a fitness advocate, a writer, and a trailblazer for generations of women who wanted more than thinness—they wanted strength, stamina, discipline, and confidence.

She made muscle beautiful. She made health aspirational. She made power feminine.

Today, when you see CrossFit champions, Olympic sprinters, and female action stars like Gal Gadot, Linda Hamilton, Tia-Clair Toomey, Annie Thorisdottir, and Sarah Sigmundsdottir—you're seeing echoes of Cory Everson.

The world where "fit is the new skinny"? Corey made it possible.

She didn't just open the door. She kicked it down and built a gym inside.

And unlike many who rose in the spotlight of early fitness media, Cory Everson kept a clean image, a disciplined life, and a humble presence. No scandals. No falls from grace. Just excellence, built day by day in the gym and in the mirror—on her own terms.

Cory Everson broke a stereotype so deeply ingrained it was almost invisible. She showed the world that muscle is not a masculine trait—it's a human one. That beauty and strength are not opposites—they are sisters. And that a woman can be powerful, graceful, feminine, and unstoppable—all at once.

She is not just the most successful female bodybuilder of all time. She is the woman who made power beautiful. And she remains—undefeated in history, and in the minds of the women she inspired.

That's Cory Everson.

Chapter 16

Pandora Peaks

The Pornstar Who Never Had Sex on Camera — The Centered Soul Behind the Centerfold

The Stereotype

Porn stars are broken souls. They're damaged, addicted, exploited. They sell their bodies, crave attention, and sacrifice dignity for a moment in the spotlight. They lack intelligence, education, grounding, or emotional stability. They do anything for money. And when the fame fades, so do they—scattered, scandalized, forgotten.

The Reality

Enter Pandora Peaks (1964-Present). The most famous big bust model of her era. The queen of a niche that ruled the 1990s and early 2000s. A woman with over 100 magazine covers, feature films, and a body so legendary it defied description—and yet, never once appeared in a hardcore scene, never once crossed the line she set for herself, and never once lost her composure, privacy, or soul.

The Obliteration of a Stereotype

In the cultural imagination, few figures are more instantly stereotyped than the adult performer. The porn star is imagined as reckless, hypersexual, undereducated, emotionally frayed. Especially during the rise of the big bust era—when hyper-exaggerated features became fetishized, commodified, and stripped of all personhood—the assumption was total: these women were just bodies. Period.

And in the middle of that landscape, right at the peak (pun intended) stood Pandora Peaks—a woman whose appearance was everything the stereotype demanded, and whose life was everything the stereotype denied.

She had breast implants of over 3,000 cubic centimeters each (nearly 14 pounds total)—among the largest in the world at the time.

She was the undisputed superstar of the big bust niche, appearing in every major adult magazine: Playboy, Hustler, Score, Gent, JUGGS, and countless others.

She featured in dozens of films and pictorials. She was the muse of legendary filmmaker Russ Meyer, who made her the star of his final film, *Pandora Peaks* (2001).

She also had a supporting role in *Striptease* (1996), opposite Demi Moore.

And yet—not once did she appear in a hardcore scene. Not once did she cross into sex work. Not once did she fall into drugs, scandal, or tabloid collapse.

And before all of that, she earned a degree in finance from the University of Georgia. She worked at Citibank. She came from a conservative Southern household. She lived with intention, saved her money, invested her earnings, and treated her work as a business—not a breakdown.

She was offered enormous amounts of money to do more—to go further. She said no, every time. And when she was at the peak of her fame, she pulled the plug.

She underwent breast reduction surgery. She retired quietly. She moved to Canada. And she disappeared—not because she was ruined, but because she was finished.

In an industry where women are often consumed and discarded, Pandora Peaks left undefeated.

Her videos were sensual, not sexual. Her performances were built around image, not intercourse. She was the only woman in adult entertainment history to become a mega-star in a sexually explicit niche without ever engaging in sex on camera.

And beyond the career, beyond the bust, beyond the myth—there was a centered soul who stayed anchored.

She didn't build an empire on exploitation. She built a life on clarity, choice, and boundary.

Pandora Peaks is a walking contradiction:

1. A sex symbol who kept her privacy.
2. A centerfold who kept her center.
3. A pornstar who never had sex on camera.
4. And perhaps, the greatest stereotype buster in the history of entertainment.

That's Pandora Peaks.

Chapter 17

James Randi

The Honest Scientific Magician Educator

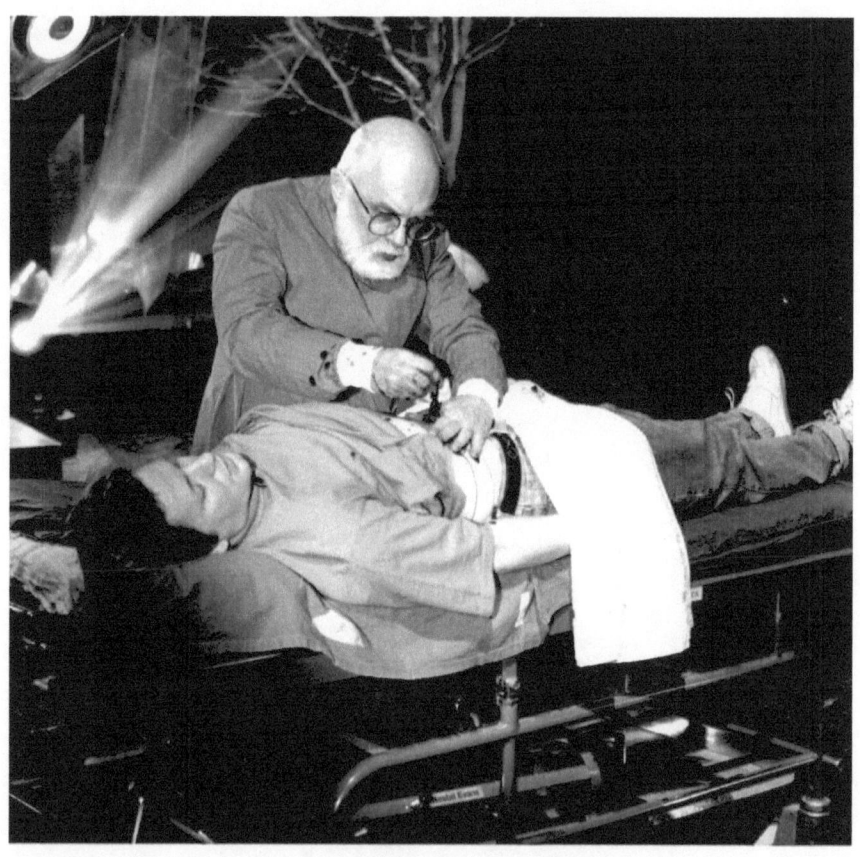

James Randi exposes a fake psychic healer — by performing the entire act himself.

The Stereotype

Magicians are con artists. They're glorified liars who profit by deceiving people. Whether dressed up as spiritualists or Vegas showmen, their trade is illusion, their goal is to blur truth, and their legacy is a trail of misled spectators. Magicians pretend to bend reality, to defy physics, to possess powers they don't have—and in doing so, they often promote fantasy over reason, trickery over truth.

The Reality

Enter James Randi (1928-2020). A world-class magician—yes. But more than that: a scientist, a skeptic, a myth-buster, and the founder of the James Randi Educational Foundation, which offered $1 million to anyone who could prove the existence of the supernatural under controlled scientific conditions. In 50 years of the challenge being open, not one person claimed the prize.

The Obliteration of a Stereotype

James Randi didn't trick people to profit. He tricked people to teach them how they were being tricked. He was the magician who pulled back the curtain. The illusionist who used his skills to expose lies—especially those who dressed up fraud as faith.

While other magicians made a living creating mystery, Randi made a mission of dismantling falsehood.

He exposed many frauds, including:

1. Psychics who claimed to speak to the dead
2. Faith healers who preyed on the sick and desperate
3. Astrologers, spoon-benders, energy-channelers, and telepaths who claimed supernatural gifts
4. And most famously, Uri Geller, the spoon-bending performer who became a media darling until Randi publicly revealed his sleight-of-hand tricks and debunked his supposed "powers"

Randi was able to spot the con because he had mastered the mechanics of illusion. He was a magician himself. A master of misdirection. But he never lied about what he was doing. He didn't claim supernatural powers—he explained the method. He didn't pretend to be divine—he advocated for the scientific method.

Through the James Randi Paranormal Challenge, he offered one of the most elegant propositions in modern science:

> **"If you can prove your powers—under fair, controlled, double-blind testing—we'll give you a million dollars."**

In 50 years, thousands of people tried. None succeeded. Because magic is illusion—and physics doesn't lie.

Randi was not a cold-hearted cynic. He didn't hate magic. He loved it. He performed it for decades with joy, elegance, and humor. But he despised the manipulation of human pain, fear, and hope for profit.

He saw through the way grief was exploited by mediums. The way desperation was preyed on by "miracle healers." The way people would believe almost anything if it was wrapped in mystery and confidence.

So, he fought back—with tools of logic, skepticism, and showmanship.

He gave TED Talks, wrote bestselling books (*Flim-Flam!*, *The Faith Healers*, *The Mask of Nostradamus*), and lectured at universities around the world. He was a frequent guest on *The Tonight Show*, where he helped Johnny Carson expose frauds, and protect viewers from scam artists.

He was revered by scientists like Carl Sagan and Richard Feynman, and inspired a generation of skeptics and rationalists.

James Randi broke the stereotype of the magician in the deepest way imaginable. He didn't hide behind smoke and mirrors. He used them to light the path toward truth. He didn't exploit mystery—he explained it. He didn't distort science—he defended it.

He didn't just pull rabbits out of hats. He pulled charlatans out of hiding, exposed them in daylight, and taught us all how not to be fooled.

James Randi wasn't a magician who fooled the world. He was the magician who warned the world.

And in doing so, he became something rarer than a wizard. He became a guardian of reason, a fighter for truth, and a man who made magic honest.

That's James Randi.

Chapter 18

Rodney Dangerfield

The Extremely Late-Blooming Jewish Comedian Who Got No Respect—Until He Got All of It

Rodney Dangerfield, starting to snowball into success. Age 51.

The Stereotype

Jewish comedians are born funny, rise fast, and dominate the spotlight with ease. From the Borscht Belt to Broadway to Netflix, they own comedy like Italians own food. They're naturals. They walk on stage and succeed. It's in the DNA. Think Jerry Seinfeld, Larry David, Woody Allen, Jon Stewart, Mel Brooks. The stereotype says: they're smart, they're sharp, and they don't have to try too hard.

The Reality

Enter Rodney Dangerfield (1921-2004). A man who got no respect—not just on stage, but in real life. A man who didn't "break through" until his mid-40s and didn't really hit it really big until almost his 60s, after decades of failure, obscurity, and backbreaking work. A man who became one of the most iconic comedians of all time—after quitting comedy for aluminum siding.

The Obliteration of a Stereotype

Born Jacob Cohen, the son of Hungarian Jewish immigrants, Rodney's childhood was a blueprint of hardship. He rarely saw his father—he once said he only saw him "two hours a year." He started writing jokes as a teenager. He tried stand-up under the name Jack Roy. And he bombed. Hard. So badly, in fact, that when he quit show business, no one noticed. His words:

> *"To give you an idea of how well I was doing at the time I quit, I was the only one who knew I quit."*

He got married. He took care of his family. He sold aluminum siding for over a decade. But the jokes never left. He wrote them between appointments. He practiced late at night. And finally—in his 40s—he came back.

This time, he created a new persona. Rodney Dangerfield: the guy who got no respect.

Self-deprecating. Disheveled. Anxious. Perfect.

And suddenly—it worked.

He appeared on The Ed Sullivan Show. Then he made it onto *The Tonight Show* with Johnny Carson—over 70 times, one of the highest totals ever. Carson loved him. America loved him. And comedy had its unlikeliest new king.

Rodney Dangerfield became a Las Vegas headliner, a bestselling author, a Hollywood star, and the owner of his own club, Dangerfield's, in New York City. His routines became classics. His albums sold millions of copies around the world. And his joke-writing speed was legendary.

But his real breakthrough came in the movie *Caddyshack* (1980). Originally written as a background character, Rodney was so electrifying on set that the script was rewritten around him. He stole the film, improvised entire scenes, and became the face of the movie.

From there, he starred in additional films like:

1. *Easy Money*
2. *Back to School*
3. *Meet Wally Sparks*
4. *Natural Born Killers* (in a dark, terrifying role that showed his range)

And he kept going—until the very end.

But what makes Rodney Dangerfield *more* than a comedian is how long it took, and how much he never gave up.

He wasn't just late-blooming—he was near-invisible for three decades. Furthermore, his life was hauntingly difficult, facing:

1. Poverty

2. Failure
3. Abandonment
4. Childhood trauma
5. Sexual abuse
6. Addiction
7. Depression

And still—he wrote. He returned. He fought through the noise. And finally, when the world was ready, he exploded into relevance.

He changed his name twice—from Jacob Cohen to Jack Roy, then to Rodney Dangerfield.
He never coasted on his ethnicity. He never played the insider. He did it the old way: joke by joke, inch by inch.

And in doing so, he shattered the stereotype that Jewish comedians just "make it." He reminded us that nothing worth building comes easy.

He didn't just break a mold. He took 30 years to climb out of one, and then made the world laugh at it.

Rodney Dangerfield is a monument to persistence. A man who found his power not in being fast—but in being real. He got no respect. Until he got all of it.

That's Rodney Dangerfield.

Chapter 19

Tony Danza

The Italian-American Tough Guy — Who Was Also the Kindest Man in the Room

The Stereotype

Italian-American men are loud, macho, temperamental, and emotionally stunted. They're brawlers, not thinkers. Lovers, not listeners. Cooks and cops and crooks and cousins. Think *The Godfather, Goodfellas, The Sopranos*. Think guidos. Muscle, chain, swagger. They're not sensitive. They don't talk about feelings. They're not stay-at-home dads. They certainly don't teach high school English or write poetry.

The Reality

Enter Tony Danza (1951-Present). Brooklyn-born. Italian to the bone. Former pro boxer. But instead of playing a tough guy for life—he flipped the whole thing upside down. He became the sweetest TV dad of the 1980s, the gentle rebel of Italian-American masculinity, and a real-life role model for compassion, literacy, and kindness.

The Obliteration of a Stereotype

Tony Danza had every ingredient to fulfill the stereotype.

1. He was born in Brooklyn, raised in a working-class Italian-American home.
2. He was a former Golden Gloves boxer.
3. He was physically built, charming, athletic.
4. Speaks with a real Brooklyn accent.
5. Loves Italian food, family, tradition.

And yet—he used all of that to subvert the mold, not reinforce it.

In the famous sitcom *Who's the Boss?*, which aired from 1984 to 1992, Danza played Tony Micelli, a widowed father and former baseball player turned live-in housekeeper. The show flipped two major gender roles:

1. The woman (played by Judith Light) was the high-powered career executive.

2. The man—the tough, Brooklyn-born, Italian-American ex-athlete—was the gentle, nurturing, apron-wearing domestic caretaker.

And he wasn't emasculated. He wasn't comedic relief. He wasn't a goofball. He was loving, emotionally intelligent, attentive, romantic, and respectful—and viewers loved him for it.

This wasn't an accident. Danza helped shape the character to reflect who he really was. He wanted to show the world that men could be strong and tender, that Italian-American men didn't have to be thugs or caricatures.

And it worked… wondrously.

Tony Danza went on to do more than act. He lived his values. Off-camera:

1. He taught high school English in Philadelphia, inspiring and mentoring struggling inner-city students.
2. He co-authored a book about the experience: *I'd Like to Apologize to Every Teacher I Ever Had*—a heartfelt, reflective, humble look at the importance of education.
3. He helped start youth literacy programs and mentored young actors.
4. He's known in Hollywood for being unfailingly polite, generous with fans, and resolutely grounded.
5. He ran multiple marathons. He boxed for charity. He promoted kindness in an industry full of ego.

He could have gone full guido. He could have taken the easy roles—mobster, thug, stereotype. And occasionally, he did—for satire. (*Don Jon*, for example, where he played a parody of the very type he spent his career dismantling.)

But his mission was clear:
Tony Danza broke the Italian-American mold—not by rejecting his heritage, but by redeeming it. He didn't distance himself

from the culture. He lived it more purely: family, loyalty, strength, warmth, humility.

And he wasn't alone.

Other Italian-Americans have broken the stereotype too:

1. Joe Mantegna – actor, playwright, thoughtful advocate
2. Martin Scorsese – intellectual, spiritual filmmaker
3. Nancy Pelosi – political powerhouse with poise
4. Frank Serpico – whistleblower, icon of integrity
5. Joe Montana – Cool Joe, the greatest quarterback in NFL history.

But none of them were built like a boxer and played a TV housekeeper with that much heart.

Tony Danza is the counterweight to every mafia caricature. He didn't play down his masculinity. He redefined it—through sweetness, sensitivity, and sincerity. He didn't shout it. He showed it.

He's the Italian-American tough guy who could cry, clean, teach, and hug—and do it all while looking cooler than anyone else on screen.

And that makes him not just a stereotype breaker—

But a gentle revolution in a leather jacket.

That's Tony Danza.

Chapter 20

Siskel and Ebert

The Non-Pretentious Film Critics — Movies for the People

The Stereotype

Film critics are pretentious. They wear turtlenecks, talk about mise-en-scène, and deconstruct plotless French films like it's a religious rite. They sneer at popcorn blockbusters, write reviews for other critics, and treat cinema like it's a sacred text that only they can interpret. They speak to the elite, not to the audience.

The Reality

Enter Gene Siskel (1946-1999) and Roger Ebert (1942-2013). Two Midwestern journalists. Two regular guys who just loved going to the movies—and told the world whether it was worth going too. They didn't sit in ivory towers. They sat in the balcony. They didn't hand out grades or lectures. They gave a thumbs up—or thumbs down. Simple. Direct. And revolutionary.

The Obliteration of a Stereotype

Siskel and Ebert were the most famous film critics in history, not because they elevated film into academia, but because they brought film back to the people... and were also of the people.

1. **Siskel:** Tall, bald, sharp, from the Chicago Tribune
2. **Ebert:** Short, round, brainy, from the Chicago Sun-Times

Both from Chicago. Both deeply opinionated. Both incapable of seeing a movie without forming an argument about it.

They disagreed constantly. They bickered, interrupted, rolled their eyes, and shot each other looks like two brothers stuck in the same seat. And it worked. It worked like magic.

Their show started on PBS, moved to syndication, and eventually became a staple of American pop culture.

Every week, they reviewed five films—not just highbrow indie gems, but mainstream, commercial movies. Blockbusters. Rom-coms. Animated films. Horror movies. Oscar contenders. B-Movies.

And their format was simple:

> *Should you spend your time and money on this movie—or not?*

Two thumbs up? Watch it.
Two thumbs down? Skip it.
One up, one down? Debate it over dinner.

They didn't analyze films to show off. They analyzed them to serve the audience.

They weren't afraid to praise what the elite dismissed. They loved movies that were fun, moving, exciting—even when they weren't "art." They celebrated:

1. Star Wars
2. Raiders of the Lost Ark
3. The Fugitive
4. The Lion King
5. Back to the Future
6. Plus, many, many more. Decades reviewing five a week, most of them non-artsy.

And they panned movies that exploited pain, trauma, or controversy for attention. They were honest. They weren't contrarians—they were curators.

They also launched careers. When no one else would cover a film, Siskel and Ebert did. When foreign films were ignored, they amplified them. When a movie had a modest budget but big ideas, they told people to go see it.

They made film criticism about the movie, not the critic. And they made it okay to love movies again—without needing a film degree or a pipe.

Siskel and Ebert didn't just review movies.
They fought about them.

Their debates, in fact, were legendary:

1. *Casino* (1994)— Siskel: "Derivative." Ebert: "One of the best films of the year."
2. *Wall Street* (1987)— Both loved it, but disagreed completely on why.
3. *Blue Velvet* (1986), *Do the Right Thing* (1989), *Rain Man* (1988)—their arguments helped shape the cultural conversation.

They weren't interested in scoring points.
They were interested in getting it right.

And they changed everything.

Every TikTok film critic, every YouTube movie reviewer, every Rotten Tomatoes contributor—they all owe a debt to Siskel and Ebert. Because before them, film criticism wasn't a conversation. It was a monologue. They turned it into a dialogue. And they let the audience in.

When Roger Ebert passed away in 2013 (many years after Siskel had, too, passed away), President Barack Obama publicly honored him, saying:

> "Roger was the movies."

And so was Gene.

Together, they made film criticism human, fun, unpretentious, and accessible. They broke the stereotype of the critic as a snob. And they replaced it with two guys sitting in a theater, arguing like friends.

Siskel and Ebert weren't just critics. They were movie lovers with microphones. And they gave the rest of us permission to love movies too—on our own terms.

That's Siskel and Ebert.

Chapter 21

Koos De la Rey

The Self-Educated General Who Defeated History's Greatest Empire

General Koos de la Rey, commanding officer of the Boers, third from left to right, circa 1901.

The Stereotype

In the modern world of warfare—drones, nuclear arsenals, satellite intelligence, cyber operations—generals are seen as hyper-educated men groomed for high command. They're graduates of war colleges, students of Clausewitz, Napoleon, Machiavelli. They memorize troop movements from the Napoleonic Wars, study logistics, and write doctoral dissertations on battlefield strategy. You can't be a world-class general, the stereotype says, unless you've read everything there is to read about war.

The Reality

Enter Koos De la Rey (1847-1914). A South African farmer. A man with no education beyond the Bible. A man who had never read a single page of military theory. A man who led an army without artillery, without tanks, without logistics, without uniforms—and yet repeatedly defeated the British Empire (the largest in history by far) at the height of its power. Not by terror. Not by chance. But by honor, genius, and instinct.

The Obliteration of a Stereotype

Born in the rugged veldt (fields) of the Transvaal in eastern South Africa, Koos de la Rey was not educated in any traditional sense. He didn't read *On War* by Von Clausewitz. He didn't go to Sandhurst. He wasn't trained by Prussian officers or British generals. He was raised on horseback. He hunted lions and leopards, survived in the wild, lived in the open, and learned everything he knew about movement, silence, and timing by watching animals and riding through Africa's unforgiving terrain.

And yet, when war broke out between the Boer Republics (his home countries) and the British Empire, it was De la Rey's name that would become legend. Not for education. Not for credentials. But for victory.

His nation—the Transvaal and its ally, the Orange Free State—had no standing army. No supply chain. No navy. No war budget. Their soldiers were farmers, hunters, clerks, and boys. The Boer system had no centralized command, no war college, no general staff.

So how did De la Rey become a general?

He was elected.
Chosen by his men, respected by his peers. Not by title, but by merit. Because he knew what to do.

He invented a military strategy comprised of organized, small, mobile fighting units made of expert horsemen and marksmen. These groups were called commandos—a word that comes from the Afrikaans language, and which has since become a universal military term and military strategy worldwide right up to the present. These commandos moved fast, struck hard, sabotaged supply lines, and disappeared before the British could respond. No uniforms. No redcoats. Just men with rifles and the will to resist.

De la Rey was a master of guerrilla warfare before guerrilla warfare had a name. He invented modern commando tactics without reading a single manual. He led night raids, disrupted supply depots, derailed trains, and captured entire British convoys.

And he did it with no maps, no communications, no artillery, and no formal hierarchy.

His army was outnumbered. Outgunned. Outresourced.
And yet—he won.

He won at Modder River, Magersfontein, and a dozen other major clashes. The British, with their warships, cannons, and empire-wide logistics, were repeatedly humiliated by De la Rey and his riders.

So, what did the British do?

They cheated.

Unable to beat him in fair battle, they turned to scorched Earth tactics and human rights abuses. They burned thousands of farms. Killed millions of livestock. Poisoned wells. And, most infamously, created the world's first concentration camps—detaining Boer women, children, and elderly civilians in brutal conditions. Over 30,000 people died in those camps.

It was genocide.

And still—De la Rey kept fighting.

He resisted surrender even when the war was lost. Even when his own home was burned. Even when his people were dying by the thousands. He fought for as long as he could. Eventually, the British offered generous terms of peace—because they knew they couldn't beat him otherwise. And only then, when offered self-rule, did he accept.

De la Rey wasn't a Clausewitzian. He wasn't a Napoleon. He wasn't a Zhukov or a General Marshall. He couldn't even read most of their names. But he was a master of terrain. A master of morale. A master of freedom.

He built his strategy not from books—but from instinct, observation, and honor.

Koos de la Rey defied everything the modern world says a general has to be. No rank. No schooling. No maps. Just a horse, a rifle, a Bible—and a mind that saw things others never could.

In the end, he lost the war. But he won history.

Because when you redefine what it means to be a general, without ever setting foot in a classroom, you don't need medals. You've already broken the mold.

That's Koos de la Rey.

Chapter 22

Isaac Asimov

The Writer Who Wrote About Everything— Except Cooking

The Stereotype

Writers pick a lane. They specialize. They build a reputation in one domain—horror, history, politics, biographies—and they stick to it. To be taken seriously, you must master one subject and milk it to the end. Step outside your field, and you're seen as diluted, scattered, unfocused. Jack of all trades, master of none. That's the warning. That's the mold.

The Reality

Enter Isaac Asimov (1920-1992). Author of over 500 books, across every conceivable subject in the Dewey Decimal System (the system used for classifying libraries)—except cooking.

Science fiction? Of course.
Physics? Yes.
History? Yes.
Mathematics? Yes.
Biblical commentary? Yes.
Children's books, literary criticism, astronomy, Shakespeare, humor, biology, etymology, neuroscience, chemistry, robotics, religion?
Yes, yes, and yes.

The Obliteration of a Stereotype

Asimov didn't just step out of the lane. He dismantled the highway and built a universe of lanes entirely his own.

He once said:

> *"Writing is simply thinking through my fingers."*

And he thought about everything... and that's no exaggeration.

Born in 1920 in Petrovichi, Russia, and raised in Brooklyn, Asimov was a prodigy of prose.

He earned a PhD in biochemistry from Columbia University and taught at Boston University—yet academia couldn't contain him. He wrote and published over 500 books, edited over 100 more, and wrote more than 90,000 letters.

He famously joked:

> "I get up in the morning and I write. Then I eat. Then I write some more. Then I go to bed."

This wasn't just productivity—it was a literary supernova.

He wrote as many as eight or nine books at a time, juggling topics ranging from genetics to Greek mythology, Shakespeare to the solar system. He had no "genre." His genre was existence.

Today, writers are taught to narrow their niche. Publishers want branding, cohesion, target demographics.

Asimov couldn't have cared less.

He wasn't a brand. He was a brain with legs, committed to demystifying knowledge and making it fun.

He wrote (among many others):
1. *The Foundation series*, which redefined science fiction
2. *The Intelligent Man's Guide to Science*, still praised for its clarity
3. Guides to the Old and New Testaments
4. A book on Shakespeare
5. Multiple volumes on the origins of words and idioms
6. And textbooks on chemistry, astronomy, biology, and math

And he didn't dabble. He mastered.
Every book he wrote was rigorous, clear, and accessible.

The stereotype says no one can do this. The stereotype says you must pick a focus or risk irrelevance.

But Asimov proved the opposite: That mastery can come not from narrowing, but from relentless curiosity.

He didn't chase prestige. He chased truth, clarity, and wonder.

He even joked that the only field he never wrote about was cooking—because he couldn't boil water. Everything else? He did. With elegance.

Asimov's bibliography includes works in:
- 000 – Computer science
- 200 – Religion
- 300 – Social sciences
- 400 – Language
- 500 – Natural sciences
- 600 – Technology
- 700 – Arts and recreation
- 800 – Literature
- 900 – History and geography

That's almost the entire Dewey Decimal System. Nine out of the ten categories.

In an age where the trend is to niche down, Asimov reminds us that the world is too big for one box. He was proof that you don't have to choose between art and science, between imagination and discipline. You can live in all of it. And if you're good enough—you can bring readers with you.

Isaac Asimov was not just a science fiction writer. He was an encyclopedia with a personality. He didn't break the mold.

He replaced it with a library.

That's Isaac Asimov.

Chapter 23

John Gierach

The Fisherman, Philosopher, and Henry David Thoreau of the Waters

The Stereotype

Fishermen are simple people. They're either industrial workers who trawl the waters with rough hands and little schooling—or bored hobbyists who drink, cast lines, and talk big while catching little. The stereotype says they're men of routine, not reflection. Workhorses or weekend warriors. But not thinkers. Not writers. Certainly not philosophers.

The Reality

Enter John Gierach (1946-2024). World-class fly fisherman. Outdoor minimalist. And the author of over twenty books on fishing that read more like Zen koans than sports manuals. A man who sees fishing not as an escape from life, but as a way to live it more deliberately.

Obliterating a Stereotype

In the popular imagination, fishermen are often reduced to caricature.

The commercial fisherman—rugged, unshaven, half-frozen, living hand to mouth.

The recreational fisherman—lazy, mildly drunk, sitting in a bass boat with a cooler and country radio.

Neither image suggests intelligence, depth, or purpose.

But for Gierach, fly fishing is art, ritual, and reflection—not sport.

Born in Minnesota, Gierach is a lifelong Midwesterner who fell in love with the stillness and rhythm of the outdoors. He chose fly fishing not for trophies, but for its aesthetic and philosophical purity.

He writes not about "winning" at fishing, but about:

1. The feel of tying your own flies by hand
2. The elegance of a well-timed cast
3. The intimacy of standing waist-deep in a cold stream, with nothing but water, wind, and instinct
4. The pleasure of catching nothing, and learning something in the process

He is, in every sense, the Henry David Thoreau of trout streams.
A man who doesn't use fishing as an excuse to drink or brag—but as a way to enter silence, listen, and think.

Gierach has said:

> *"Fishing is not an escape from life, but often a deeper immersion into it."*

He doesn't fish for food, money, or ego. He fishes for clarity. And in his books—like *Trout Bum, Still Life with Brook Trout, No Shortage of Good Days*, and *All Fishermen Are Liars*—he writes with humor, depth, and gentle precision.

He is a philosopher with a fly rod, a man who builds his own gear, avoids luxury, and often fishes alone—not for isolation, but for perspective.

In a world obsessed with productivity and performance, Gierach writes about subjects like the value of doing something slowly, the joy of not measuring success by outcome and the quiet satisfaction of a cast that goes unnoticed by everything but the river

He breaks the stereotype not by shouting it down—but by living the opposite.

He doesn't shout. He listens. He doesn't chase fish. He lets the water offer what it will.

Most fishermen are never taken seriously as thinkers. They're background noise. But Gierach shows that a fisherman can also be:

1. A writer of literary beauty
2. A student of nature's philosophy
3. A minimalist
4. A spiritualist
5. A master of presence

He doesn't cast lines for status. He casts them to align himself with something ancient, patient, and eternal.

John Gierach is not just a fisherman. He's a reader of rivers, a writer of silence, and a man who reminds us that stillness is not laziness—but wisdom wearing waders.

In a world that rushes to consume, he simply stands in the water and listens. And in doing so, he becomes the most meditative stereotype breaker of them all.

That's John Gierach.

Chapter 24

Anatoly Tarasov

The Soviet Innovator Who Transformed Hockey with Ballet, Chess, and Finesse

In just a few years, the USSR went from having no hockey, to dominating the world stage. Here seen beating Canada, considered the best in the world.

The Stereotype

Hockey is a game of brute force. It's a sport for enforcers, brawlers, goons. It's played with fists, speed, shoulder checks, and grit. Strategy is an afterthought. Innovation is nonexistent. In hockey, you win with either raw talent or overwhelming physicality. Coaches just recycle old systems. It's not a game you "reinvent."

The Reality

Enter Anatoly Tarasov (1918-1995). The founding father of Soviet hockey, the biggest sports dynasty of all time (and it's not even close). A man who turned Canada's game into Russia's masterpiece. A man who studied ballet, chess, physics, and psychology—and in doing so, redesigned a sport the world thought couldn't be changed.

Obliterating a Stereotype

From the 1950s to the fall of the Soviet Union in 1991, the USSR national hockey team was the most dominant team in the history of organized sports... and its no exaggeration. Neither the dynasties of the Boston Celtics, Chicago Bulls, New England Patriots, Cleveland Browns, New York Yankees, or any other team in any other country even comes close.

They won nearly every international tournament they entered. They secured 9 consecutive world championship gold medals from 1963 to 1971. They won 7 Olympic golds between 1956 and 1988. And in exhibition games, they obliterated Team Canada, Team USA, and even NHL All-Star lineups.

In a sport founded in Canada and ruled by the NHL, the Soviets didn't just compete—they made the game look outdated.

But their secret wasn't talent. It was Tarasov.

A former player, a military man, and a theorist of the highest order, Tarasov was given the task of building Soviet hockey from nothing. Russia had no history in the sport. No infrastructure. No legends. So, Tarasov did what innovators do best—he looked elsewhere.

He studied:
1. Chess: for spacing, anticipation, control.
2. Ballet: for footwork, balance, fluidity.
3. Mathematics and rhythm: for passing patterns and timing.

4. Team cohesion: for psychological edge.

He rejected the Canadian model of aggression and individualism. He refused to rely on enforcers, stars, or brute force. Instead, he created a game that was fast, precise, elegant, and relentless.

His philosophy was clear:

"Hockey is not about violence. It's about movement. It's about unity. It's about beauty."

His training programs were legendary, with activities that had never been seen before in the sport:

1. Players practiced synchronized skating, like figure skaters.
2. They ran ballet drills to improve balance.
3. They passed the puck without looking, to build intuition.
4. And every play was rehearsed like a line of choreography—fluid, smart, brutal only in its efficiency.

The result?

A team with no stars, no egos, no drop-off. Just a machine of human motion that left other teams exhausted, bewildered, and destroyed.

In one of the most famous international clashes, the Soviet team beat the NHL All-Stars 6–0 in 1979, stunning fans and analysts alike. But that was only a glimpse of who they were.

They crushed Team Canada 7–3 in 1976 and in 1981 (even with Wayne Gretzky --- by a score of 8-1). And they even beat Team Canada, at their very best, by a score of 6-5 in the 1987 Canada Cup with a Canadian squad that had 13 hall of famers including Gretzky at his best as well as legendary players like Mario Lemieux, Mark Messier, Steve Yzerman, Dale Hawerchuck, Glenn Anderson, Michel Goulet, and many more.

In essence, they dominated every nation, every rink, every era—except for the one blip: the Miracle on Ice in 1980. Even then, they walked away with silver, not collapse.

No other dynasty in sports history—not the Bulls, not the Patriots, not the Yankees, not Brazil in soccer—has matched that level of statistical and strategic dominance for so long.

Tarasov didn't rely on fancy equipment. He didn't chase celebrity. He didn't allow fighting on his teams. He banned showboating, trash-talking, and individual celebration.

He trained his players to see the game as a collective ballet of blades and thought. And that's exactly what they became.

Coaches, by nature, aren't expected to innovate. They're expected to optimize. But Tarasov broke that mold.

He wasn't just a coach. He was an architect of motion. He was a tactician who thought like a scientist. And he changed a sport built on muscle into a theater of movement and intelligence.

Anatoly Tarasov wasn't celebrated much in the West. Too Soviet. Too strange. Too "different."

But make no mistake:

He is to hockey what Naismith is to basketball, what Bill James is to baseball, what Red Auerbach is to coaching.

He took a borrowed game and made it a Russian art form. He turned hockey into ballet on ice, with chessboard logic and military execution. And in doing so, he shattered the idea that sports are only won with fists and fire.

Sometimes, they're won with grace.

That's Anatoly Tarasov.

Chapter 25

Bill James

The Meatpacking Security Guard Who Revolutionized Baseball Without Ever Setting Foot on the Field

The Stereotype

Security guards don't innovate. They're underpaid placeholders. Rent-a-cops. Bored men with clipboards and radios. They don't change the world. They don't make headlines. They certainly don't redesign a national pastime. And in sports—especially baseball—true innovation comes from players, coaches, insiders, not graveyard-shift nobodies behind a desk.

The Reality

Enter Bill James (1949-Present). Security guard at a pork processing plant. Night shift worker. Self-educated statistical savant. And the man who redesigned baseball—from a small office, with nothing but paper, a calculator, and obsessive precision.

Obliterating a Stereotype

If you've seen or read *Moneyball*, you know the ripple effect. Bill James didn't just analyze baseball—he rewrote it. And he did it by questioning everything the game held sacred.

And if you haven't read or seen it, here's the shocking story: For over 100 years, baseball lived and died by one statistic: batting average. It was treated as gospel. But James, poring over decades of data during long, quiet nights in his security booth, saw something else.

On-base percentage mattered more. The best players weren't necessarily the flashiest—they were the ones who just. kept. getting. on. base.

He dug deeper. He invented new metrics. He created sabermetrics—a science of baseball performance. And he showed that a team of mathematically valuable players—even if they looked unremarkable—could dominate the game.

Bill James didn't come from the majors. He wasn't a scout. He wasn't a coach. He didn't even play. He wasn't connected to the industry. He was a nobody with numbers.

And he published them anyway—in a series of self-published newsletters called *the Baseball Abstracts*.

They were detailed, obsessive, and ignored by almost everyone—until they weren't.

Enter Billy Beane, general manager of the Oakland Athletics.

Beane and his Harvard-educated assistant read James's work and implemented it. They built a low-budget team based on sabermetric values—not hype. And they nearly took that team to the World Series... twice.

The story was so revolutionary, it became *Moneyball*, a bestselling book and later a film starring none other than Brad Pitt and Jonah Hill.

But behind the scenes, Bill James's theories were the engine.

Eventually, James was hired by the Boston Red Sox as a senior advisor. And in 2004, that team broke the "Curse of the Bambino", winning their first World Series in 86 years. They would go on to build a dynasty—with Bill James's data behind every major move.

The transformation was so dramatic, it became cultural:

1. Every team in Major League Baseball now uses sabermetrics.
2. Analysts are prized as much as scouts.
3. And the assumptions of 150 years have been permanently overturned.

All because a man who "should've just been a security guard" refused to accept what everyone else believed was true.

But it wasn't easy. He was laughed at, dismissed, and ignored. He had no credibility, no credentials, and no welcome mat at the door.

People said:

> "You're a security guard. What the hell do you know?"

His answer? Everything.

Bill James is one of the greatest stereotype breakers in modern sports history. He didn't just rewrite baseball. He proved that outsiders can see more clearly than insiders. That data matters more than tradition. And that a man with a quiet mind and a relentless method can change everything—without ever putting on a uniform.

There is a before and after in baseball. The turning point isn't a player. It's not a manager. It's not even a game.

It's Bill James, sitting alone in a meatpacking plant, surrounded by silence and statistics—
and quietly reprogramming the national pastime.

That's Bill James.

Chapter 26

Steve Reeves

The Bodybuilder Who Hated Showing Off His Body

The Stereotype

Bodybuilders are narcissists. They flex in the mirror, wear tank tops in the snow, and treat the gym like a temple to themselves. They show off, pose, and crave attention. Without their muscles, they are nothing. They use steroids, flaunt their physiques, and build a personality out of biceps.

The Reality

Enter Steve Reeves (1926-2000). Mr. America. Mr. World. Mr. Universe. The man with the best body on Earth—and the least interest in showing it.

Obliterating A Stereotype

Steve Reeves is one of the founding fathers of modern bodybuilding. Alongside Eugen Sandow, Joe Weider, Jack LaLanne, Joe Gold, and Arnold Schwarzenegger, he forms part of the pantheon of the sport's pioneers.

But unlike the rest, he didn't flex for fame. He didn't promote supplements. He didn't court attention.

He built a masterpiece of a body—and hid it in oversized sweatsuits.

Born in 1926 in rural Montana, near the Canadian border, Reeves grew up on hard work and heartbreak. His father, a farmhand, died when Steve was 10. But this only pushed him to work harder.

He served in World War II in the Philippines, before rising to become the natural bodybuilding champion of the world.

He won:

1. Mr. America (1947)
2. Mr. World (1948)
3. Mr. Universe (1950)

All without steroids. All before performance-enhancing drugs invaded the sport. All by training three times a week, full-body style, and living with balance.

Then came Hollywood.

Reeves was cast as Hercules, and he became the highest-paid actor in Europe. He then starred in swords-and-sandals epics across Italy and France—in films like *Goliath, Sandokan, Romulus,* and *The Last Days of Pompeii*—all with a physique so extraordinary it barely looked real.

And yet—he still didn't flaunt it. He avoided the spotlight. He wore long sleeves. He didn't do magazine shoots for vanity. He avoided the showboating culture of modern fitness entirely.

Steve Reeves didn't need attention. He had discipline. And that was enough.

In an era where bodybuilding was becoming synonymous with ego, drugs, and obsession, Reeves stood for something else entirely: *Natural achievement. Quiet excellence. Strength with restraint.*

He wasn't just a star. He was a philosopher of form—a man who believed that your body should speak for itself. And if it didn't? You shouldn't be screaming anyway.

He later became an author, publishing bestsellers on natural bodybuilding, fitness, and longevity. He warned against steroids. He promoted balance. He lived humbly.

He could have ridden fame for decades. Instead, he walked away—healthy, accomplished, unscathed. Because he didn't just want to be a strong man. He wanted to be a complete one.

And the punchline?

Steve Reeves had the greatest body in the world—and he didn't need to show it to anyone. Because he already knew it.

That was his legacy. Strength without vanity. Discipline without ego. Greatness without noise.

That's Steve Reeves.

Chapter 27

Sam Walton

The Billionaire Who Drove an Old Truck and Wore Overalls

The Office of the Richest man in the World.

The Stereotype

Billionaires flaunt their wealth. They live in mansions, fly private, speak from stages, and tweet their way into immortality. They want to be admired. They want to be seen. And if they act humble, it's for branding—never because they actually are.

The Reality

Enter Sam Walton (1918-1992). Founder of Walmart. Creator of the largest retail empire in human history. The richest man in the world during his time (and if he were still alive, his fortune would still be the largest in the world by far). And yet—he dressed like a farmer, drove an old pickup truck with his dogs in the back, and wore a worn ball cap like he just got off shift at the feed store.

Obliterating the Hot Shot Billionaire Stereotype

Sam Walton was born in 1918, in rural Missouri. He grew up during the Great Depression, where the value of a dollar wasn't theoretical—it was survival. His father died in a farming accident. He served in World War II. And he came back with a belief so simple it could be printed on a receipt:

Give the customer more for less.

He didn't invent retail—but he revolutionized it. He brought scale, logistics, rural access, and price efficiency to levels never seen before. He created Walmart. Then Sam's Club. Then a logistical empire so refined it would become the model for modern retail distribution.

And through it all, he kept asking:

"How do we serve better?"

Sam Walton didn't show off. He hated being called the richest man in the world. He flew his own tiny single engine propeller plane—not because it was luxurious, but because he was a licensed pilot and needed to visit his stores.

And that plane was so old and small that colleagues joked it ran on a lawn mower engine.

And when he wasn't on the plane, he drove an old red pick-up that has since become legendary. When someone suggested he buy a Rolls Royce instead, he replied:

"Where the hell would I put my dogs?"

He lived in a modest house in Bentonville, Arkansas. He wore denim, flannel, and baseball caps. He gave few interviews. He never postured. And he never stopped working.

Sam Walton wasn't interested in image. He was interested in improvement.

He created a company that didn't serve luxury buyers—it served working people. And Walmart still does. It's a recession-proof business because it's built on the backbone of frugality.

"Save money. Live better." That's not marketing. That's his worldview.

And yet, despite being the richest man in the world, he lived like he never left the town square. He didn't need an audience. He didn't need adulation. He needed work, humility, and purpose. Because he knew the world didn't need another rich man pretending to be humble.

It needed a humble man who happened to be rich.

Today, billionaires race to space. They flaunt their jets, their watches, their brands. They want to be remembered. They want to be followed. They want to be adored.

Sam Walton? He just wanted to know how aisle three was doing in the Fort Smith location.

He didn't just change business. He changed access. He changed rural economies. He changed retail logistics. And he did it without ever chasing a spotlight.

Sam Walton built the largest company in the world by revenue. But he never built a mansion for himself.

He didn't want to be a brand. He wanted to be better.

The punchline? He was the richest man on Earth—and still the kind of man who'd pick up his own change if he dropped it.

That's not image. That's legacy.

That's Sam Walton.

Chapter 28

General George C. Marshall

The Quiet General Who Led the Greatest War in History Without Saying a Word

General George C. Marshall at the Yalta Conference in 1945, planning the world post WW2 standing quietly in the background (arrow pointing at him) as Churchill, Roosevelt, and Stalin take center stage — a reflection of his humility and belief in collective achievement.

The Stereotype

Generals are loud (1880-1959). They scream. They demand. They crave power, glory, and reverence. They think in orders and operate in ego. They walk with a strut, speak in soundbites, and view humility as weakness. Think Patton. Think MacArthur. Think Napoleon. Think every general in every movie ever made.

The Reality

Enter General George C. Marshall. The highest-ranking American military officer of World War II. The architect of Allied victory. And the least known, least quoted, least self-promoting man in the room.

Obliterating a Stereotype

When most people think of World War II generals, they think of the names with flair:

1. **General Dwight D. Eisenhower** – the Supreme Commander who became President
2. **General Douglas MacArthur** – the dramatist of the Pacific, the man with the hat and the pipe
3. **General George Patton** – the loud-mouthed tank genius with a pearl-handled pistol

But none of them held the rank, the influence, or the weight of General George C. Marshall.

Marshall was Chief of Staff of the U.S. Army from 1939 to 1945. He was Eisenhower's boss, MacArthur's boss, Patton's boss. He coordinated both the European and Pacific theaters.

He oversaw the largest military expansion in U.S. history, from fewer than 200,000 troops to over 8 million. And he did it all without ever commanding a battle himself.

He didn't need to. Because Marshall was strategy, discipline, and moral strength incarnate.

He held a PhD-level command of logistics, and was responsible for coordinating the most complex supply chain in history—moving weapons, tanks, rations, and men across two oceans, two continents, and a hundred fronts.

He was so committed to fairness that when President Roosevelt offered to name him Supreme Commander of the D-Day invasion, Marshall refused to influence the decision.
He told FDR:

"You must make the choice, Mr. President, based on what's best for the war effort."

Roosevelt picked Eisenhower. Marshall didn't sulk. He just kept working.

When World War II ended, Marshall didn't write a memoir. He didn't tour for speaking gigs. He didn't ask for medals. He walked the halls of the Pentagon in quiet reflection, too moved to celebrate.

And then—he went back to work.

As Secretary of State under Truman, Marshall designed The Marshall Plan—the post-war economic recovery effort that rebuilt Europe, prevented mass starvation, stabilized democracies, and stopped the rise of communism in Western Europe.

He hated the name. He wanted it to be called "The European Recovery Program". But Truman overruled him.

He was also a founding architect of NATO. A man who believed that peace came from unity, discipline, and readiness—not from bluster.

He was offered the presidency. He refused. He was offered parades. He declined. He was offered headlines. He deflected.

Instead, he rode horses. He rowed down rivers. He kept a low profile and lived his creed: service before self.

In a world of swaggering generals, George Marshall stood alone.

He didn't yell. He didn't threaten. He didn't perform. He executed. He didn't need to raise his voice. Because when Marshall spoke—everyone listened.

He won World War II. He rebuilt Europe. He shaped the Cold War defense doctrine. And then he faded into quiet anonymity—as if that were the point all along.

And the punchline? He was the most powerful general in the world—because he was the only one who never wanted to be.

That's not just rare. That's revolutionary.

That's General George C. Marshall.

Chapter 29

Arnold Schwarzenegger

The Bodybuilder Polymath Who Left Da Vinci Biting the Dust

The Stereotype

Bodybuilders are dumb. They live in the gym, stare at the mirror, worship their biceps, and measure their worth by reps, calories, and inches. They're narcissists, meatheads, obsessed with appearance, and often incapable of thinking beyond protein shakes and posing routines. They're not thinkers. Not leaders. Not strategists.

The Reality

Enter Arnold Schwarzenegger (1947-Present). Fifteen-time world champion bodybuilder. World-class powerlifter with a 2,000-pound total. Golden Globe–winning actor and the highest-paid star in Hollywood history (and it's not even close). Multi-Bestselling author. Multi-millionaire entrepreneur. Governor of California—the fifth-largest economy on Earth. And one of the most accomplished polymaths to walk the planet… ever.

Obliterating a Stereotype

When you think of the phrase "renaissance man," a bodybuilder isn't the first image that comes to mind. But Arnold Schwarzenegger didn't just blur that line—he annihilated it.

Born in Austria in 1947, raised in post-war poverty, Arnold entered bodybuilding at 15, won Mr. Universe at 20, and would go on to win:

1. 7 Mr. Olympias (the highest-level bodybuilding competition in the world)
2. 5 Mr. Universes
3. And over 15 world championships

No nonsense—just relentless training, discipline, and vision. And then? He walked away from it all—at the peak of his sport.

Why? Because bodybuilding was just the beginning.

Arnold had already become a millionaire through business before he ever stepped onto a movie set, and in the subsequent years, he became even more successful.

1. He co-owned a very profitable construction company in California.
2. He invested in real estate and retail chains all throughout America.
3. He helped bring the Hummer to the civilian market.
4. He co-founded Planet Hollywood.
5. He owned gyms.
6. He owned brands.
7. He launched merchandising lines and global newsletters.
8. He launched the largest sports festival event in the world by number of athletes – the Arnold Classic (larger even than the Olympics)

He understood branding before branding became culture. And in the meantime, while he did all that, came Hollywood.

He became:

1. The highest-paid actor of all time.
2. A box office juggernaut with roles in *The Terminator, Terminator 2, Predator, Total Recall, True Lies, Twins* and many more.
3. A surprising Golden Globe winner for *Stay Hungry*
4. A producer and director
5. A crossover comedy icon

And he made close to a billion million in earnings, adjusted for inflation—without losing his humility or drive.

Then came politics.

Arnold Schwarzenegger became Governor of California. Reelected twice. He led the world's fifth-largest economy through massive budgetary reform, bipartisan legislation, massive infrastructure development, and sweeping environmental policy.

He championed:

1. Renewable energy with policies such as the "Million solar roofs initiative" to replace fossil fuels.
2. Infrastructure - Investing 60 billion dollars to rebuild California's infrastructure.
3. Fiscal responsibility
4. Social Reform

He proved he could lead people, not just entertain them. And while he was doing all of that?

He was writing bestselling books. Delivering motivational speeches. Running global fitness campaigns. And mentoring generations of athletes, entrepreneurs, and leaders.

Arnold isn't just a renaissance man. He's a polymath in the truest sense:

World-class mastery in unrelated disciplines—earned, not claimed.

Bodybuilding.
Acting.
Business.
Politics.
Writing.
Philosophy.
Leadership.

And all of it with a thick Austrian accent, a 57-inch chest, and more charisma than a dozen CEOs combined.

He defied not just one stereotype—but ten at once. And he did it all while being judged at first glance as "just a muscle guy."

The punchline?

He walked into the world as a bodybuilder—and ended up conquering it like a philosopher king.

That's not a career.
That's a blueprint.

That's Arnold Schwarzenegger.

Chapter 30

John Bogle

The Saint of Wall Street

The Stereotype

Wall Street is a shark tank. It's full of fast-talking hustlers who sell you what you don't need, pocket your fees, and disappear when the market turns. They speak in jargon, bury you in fine print, and treat your life savings like poker chips. From Bernie Madoff to Allen Stanford, from Jordan Belfort to countless nameless fund managers, Wall Street's reputation is clear: They win. You lose.

The Reality

Enter John Bogle (1929-2019). The founder of Vanguard, the largest investment firm in the world, with over $8 trillion in assets under management. The creator of the index fund. And the only man in modern financial history who built a fortune by giving away the profits.

Obliterating a Stereotype

Wall Street has long been seen as a predator's paradise, and rightfully so.

Most investment firms charge layers of fees:

1. 1-2% to manage your money
2. Entry fees
3. Exit fees
4. Management fees
5. Hidden fees

And all of that is before you make a dime.

John Bogle changed all of that.

He built a firm where:

1. You keep your money
2. You own the firm (Vanguard is owned by its shareholders)

3. And your returns are driven by the market—not by a manager trying to beat it

He introduced the index fund. A simple concept:

Buy every stock in the market, keep your costs low, and hold for the long haul.

That idea was laughed at when he launched it in 1976.
Brokers called it "Bogle's folly."
Wall Street ignored him.
But Bogle didn't care.

He knew that most actively managed funds underperform the market. And he also knew another big problem was fees. So, he built a system that attacked both. He bought the market as a whole via the index funds, and charged as little as 0.03% annually— to his clients. That's $3 a year for every $10,000 invested.

Compare that to the typical 2% fee on Wall Street—$200 per $10,000.

Bogle let your money grow. Everyone else just fed on it.

But he didn't stop with the math.
He made investing accessible to the little guy.
1. Minimum investment: $1
2. No commissions
3. No pressure
4. No gimmicks

And then he told you what to do:

"Buy the whole market. Hold it. Stay the course."

That's it. No prediction. No panic. Just principled patience.

Bogle's legacy isn't just technical. It's moral.

He believed in transparency, fiduciary responsibility, and democratized wealth-building.

And if that wasn't enough, he also wrote 15 books, including the iconic *The Little Book of Common Sense Investing*, which explains his philosophy and strategy in the simplest way possible.

He lectured everywhere. He kept Vanguard's headquarters in Pennsylvania—far from the vanity of Wall Street. He lived simply. He gave away generously. And he always warned about the dangers of overconfidence, overtrading, and overcharging.

Bogle didn't chase billions. He chased efficiency. He chased fairness. He chased justice in finance.

And his impact?
Unmatched.
1. Vanguard has over 25 million customers.
2. It has outperformed nearly every active fund.
3. It manages more money than almost any nation on Earth.

And it all started because John Bogle refused to take more than he needed.

The punchline?

He became the most ethical man in the most unethical industry—and beat them at their own game.

That's not investing.
That's a revolution in trust.

That's John Bogle.

Chapter 31

Mr. Rogers

The Multimillionaire Who Was Also the Nicest Man in the World

The Stereotype

Millionaires and billionaires are ruthless. They made their money by stepping on others, cutting corners, chasing power. They flaunt it. They obsess over it. They wear the suit, ride the private jet, and chase the spotlight. And if they appear humble, it's a marketing strategy, not a state of being. Behind every great fortune, there's a crime—or at least an ego.

The Reality

Enter Fred Rogers (1928-2003). Also known as Mr. Rogers. A classically trained pianist. A Presbyterian minister. A children's television host. A man worth many millions of dollars, born into wealth, who could have done anything—and chose to do something rare: To be kind. Without agenda. Without irony. Without exception.

Obliterating A Stereotype

Fred Rogers came from a wealthy family. He was already a millionaire before *Mister Rogers' Neighborhood* ever aired. He didn't need to work. He didn't need to hustle. He could have coasted. Instead, he devoted his entire life to children's emotional and psychological well-being.

Mister Rogers' Neighborhood wasn't flashy. No special effects. No action. No loud noises.
Just a man in a sweater, talking about feelings, fears, empathy, and love.

He addressed:
1. Death
2. Divorce
3. Bullying
4. Self-worth
5. Race, disability, war, peace, and everything in between

He showed children how to process pain. He showed adults how to speak softly and mean it. He made kindness feel revolutionary.

But what really shatters the stereotype is how he handled success.

He turned down millions of dollars in commercial offers. He refused to commercialize his show or license his characters. He didn't want children to confuse his messages with merchandise.

PBS offered him enough to live comfortably. That was all he needed. Because money was never the point. Mission was.

He once said:

> *"Fame is a four-letter word. And like tape or zoom or face or pain or life or love, what ultimately matters is what you do with it."*

And what he did with it was create a model of moral clarity.

He worked tirelessly. He exercised every day. He responded to fan mail—by hand. He stayed in the same modest house with his wife until the end of his life. He spoke the same way off camera as on. And even in his final days, dying of stomach cancer, he apologized to others for being a burden.

People didn't believe he was real. Even journalists suspected it was an act.

A very famous interview (which inspired the Tom Hanks film *A Beautiful Day in the Neighborhood*) featured a hardened reporter trying to find the "real" Fred Rogers beneath the persona—only to discover... there wasn't a persona.

He was the real thing.

In a world where power almost always distorts goodness, Mr. Rogers stood as living proof that you could be:
1. Rich and humble
2. Famous and private
3. Influential and invisible
4. Powerful and gentle

He didn't just break the stereotype. He made kindness a kind of strength.

He refused to run his show anywhere other than PBS. He wanted it to be free, safe, untainted by advertising. He didn't need the spotlight. He just wanted to help people feel okay in their own skin.

And he succeeded.

When he died in 2003, millions mourned. Not because he was flashy. But because he meant what he said. Every time.

> *"You've made this day a special day, just by being you. There's no one in the whole world like you, and I like you just the way you are."*

The punchline?

Mr. Rogers had millions in the bank—and still treated everyone like they mattered more than he did.

That's not branding.
That's grace.

That's Fred Rogers.

Chapter 32

Bob Ross

The Drill Sergeant Who Chose to Whisper to the World

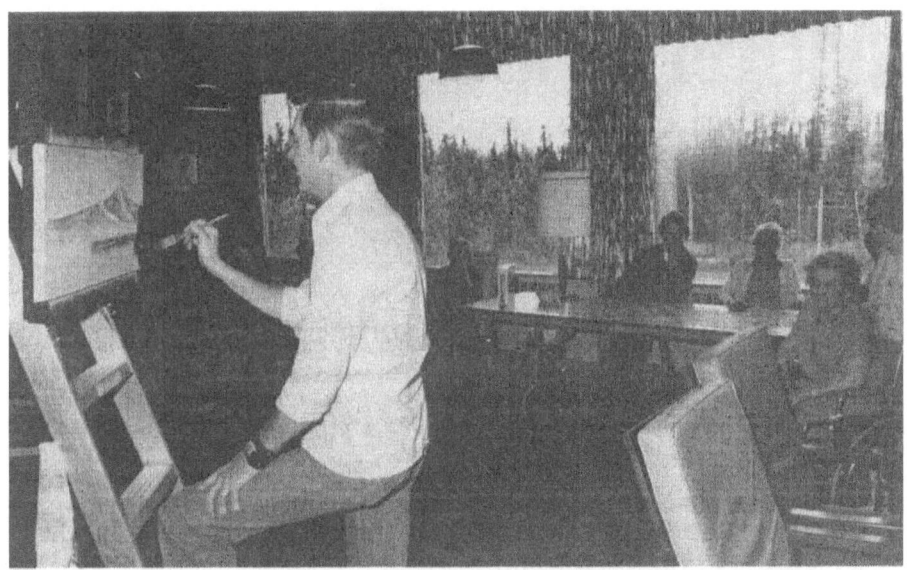

Bob Ross, long before the afro and TV fame, serving as a U.S. Air Force sergeant in Alaska, teaching veterans and civilians to paint.

The Stereotype

Drill sergeants are screamers. They bark. They punish. They break you down to build you up—but mostly, they break. They're intense, commanding, aggressive, sometimes even cruel. Their image is cemented in military lore: crew cuts, pressed uniforms, spit-flecked shouting, and eyes that never blink. They don't smile. They don't soften. And they certainly don't paint.

The Reality

Enter Bob Ross (1942-1995). One of the kindest, most soothing presences in television history. Host of *The Joy of Painting*, where for 11 years and 403 episodes, he whispered us through forests of happy little trees and friendly little clouds—while sporting an iconic afro and a voice like warm chamomile... and yes, a former United States Air Force Drill Instructor.

Obliterating a Stereotype

What few knew was that Bob Ross spent 20 years in the United States Air Force, rising to the rank of Master Sergeant. And he was indeed a drill instructor... and not a nice one who spoke of the joys of life or painting or happy clouds. No... He trained recruits. He gave orders. He enforced discipline. He lived the life of the shouting stereotype.

And then—he walked away from it all.

Ross once said:

> *"I was the guy who made you scrub the latrine. The guy who made you make your bed. The guy who screamed at you for being late. And I decided that when I left the military, I would never raise my voice again."*

And he never did.

He traded his crew cut for a halo of curls. His drill voice for a whisper. His uniform for an open collar. And his battlefield became a canvas of peace.

After retiring from the military, Ross took up painting full-time. He studied under Bill Alexander, a German-born painter who taught the "wet-on-wet" technique—perfect for painting landscapes in real time.

Ross mastered it—and then made it his own.

In 1983, *The Joy of Painting* premiered on PBS. It was low-budget. Low-tech. But it became an American institution.

Viewers didn't just watch Bob Ross paint—they felt him. He wasn't teaching art. He was teaching calm, reverence, presence, and joy.

He painted:
1. Majestic Alaskan wildernesses
2. Snow-capped mountains
3. Lakes of mirror stillness
4. Cabins tucked into serenity

And every brushstroke was a quiet rebellion against the world he had come from.

Ross didn't chase attention. He didn't profit from fame. He donated most of his paintings to charity, hospitals, and PBS stations. He lived modestly, with his squirrels, his solitude, and his love of peace.

People often assumed Bob Ross was naive. But the truth is far more powerful: He knew what the world could be like—and chose, instead, to create something gentler.

He wasn't blind to cruelty. He had trained men for war, many of them for Vietnam. He simply chose not to echo that intensity into the rest of his life.

Bob Ross didn't just whisper to a canvas. He whispered to a culture growing too loud. He reminded us that not all strength needs to shout. That not all leaders need to dominate. That not all pasts define the future.

He wasn't just painting trees. He was painting peace.

The punchline?

He trained soldiers by yelling—and healed the world by whispering. That's not just contrast. That's transformation.

That's Bob Ross.

Chapter 33

Bob Woodward

The Journalist Who Changed History

The Stereotype

Journalists report on history—they don't make it. They observe. They summarize. They get the facts wrong, spin the rest, and call it breaking news. They chase headlines, not justice. They're biased, performative, and ultimately forgettable. In a world of power, journalists are the audience—not the actors.

The Reality

Enter Bob Woodward (1943-Present). Reporter for The Washington Post. Co-author of the Watergate investigation. And the man who toppled a sitting president—not with weapons, not with influence, but with a notepad and the truth.

Obliterating a Stereotype

In 1972, a break-in at the Watergate Complex in Washington, D.C.—home to the Democratic National Committee—seemed like just another burglary. Five men were caught wiretapping phones and stealing documents. The story should've ended there.

But it didn't. Because Bob Woodward refused to let it go.

Together with fellow reporter Carl Bernstein, Woodward began to dig. They connected the burglars to members of Nixon's re-election campaign. They traced cash trails. They interviewed sources.

They chased dead ends and watched phones click under surveillance. They met anonymous informants in underground parking garages—including "Deep Throat," who would later be revealed as Mark Felt, Deputy Director of the FBI.

And with each article, the walls closed in.

They didn't just uncover the break-in. They uncovered the conspiracy behind it—a web of obstruction, hush money, and presidential abuse of power.

They proved that President Richard Nixon knew. That he lied. That he directed others to lie. That he abused the full power of his office to cover it up.

Woodward and Bernstein didn't publish opinions. They published facts.

And those facts brought down the most powerful man in the world.

In August 1974, after two years of relentless reporting, Nixon resigned the presidency—the first and only U.S. president ever to do so.

That wasn't punditry. That wasn't spin. That was Bob Woodward, and a typewriter.

But Watergate wasn't the end. It was just the beginning.

Bob Woodward went on to write over 20 books, including:
1. *The Brethren (*on the inner workings of the Supreme Court.
2. *Plan of Attack*, *Bush at War*, and *State of Denial* (on the wars in Iraq and Afghanistan)
3. *Obama's Wars*
4. *Fear* and *Rage* (on the Trump presidency)
5. *Peril* (on the Biden transition and January 6th)

Each book was based on hundreds of hours of interviews, documented sources, deep investigation. No fluff. No shortcuts.

He exposed:
1. Secrets in the White House
2. Inner turmoil at the Pentagon
3. Failures in crisis management
4. Fault lines in democracy itself

And he did it without ego, without noise, and without ever chasing celebrity.

In essence, Bob Woodward changed the role of the journalist.

He wasn't a talking head. He didn't perform outrage. He quietly revealed what power didn't want known—and did so with discipline, accuracy, and steel nerves.

In a profession now overrun by hot takes and anonymous tweets, Woodward is a monument to real reporting.

He is still writing. Still publishing. Still holding power to account.

He once said:

"The central dilemma in journalism is that you don't know what you don't know."

And yet—he found out anyway.

The punchline?

Bob Woodward didn't just report history—he made it blink.

That's not journalism as we know it. That's journalism as it was meant to be.

That's Bob Woodward.

Chapter 34

Ted Koppel

The In-Depth, Ethical Anchorman Who Refused to Sensationalize the News

The Stereotype

Journalists are sensationalists. They scream. They push agendas. They twist stories for ratings. They're not interested in the truth—they're interested in their truth. In what sells. In what provokes. The modern anchor isn't a public servant—they're a performer. A mouthpiece. A manipulator.

The Reality

Enter Ted Koppel (1940-Present). Host of NBC's *Nightline*. One of the most respected newsmen in the history of American television. And a journalist who, for over three decades, delivered the news quietly, ethically, and without sensationalism.

Obliterating a Stereotype

Ted Koppel is what happens when a man takes truth seriously—and never lets go. For over 25 years, he anchored *Nightline*, one of the most enduring and respected programs in the history of network news.

He covered:
1. The Iranian hostage crisis
2. The AIDS epidemic
3. The Chernobyl disaster
4. The Challenger explosion
5. Multiple wars, elections, political scandals, and social shifts

And through it all, he never raised his voice.

He was calm. Measured. Precise. And relentlessly objective.

He didn't "both sides" every issue—he curated the right sources, the right experts, and the right tone. He wasn't interested in drama. He was interested in clarity.

When others shouted, Koppel listened. When others speculated, Koppel verified. When others hyped panic, Koppel explained with restraint.

During the Chernobyl disaster, when many American networks warned of radioactive clouds drifting to the U.S., Koppel brought on scientists who calmly explained that any radiation reaching the U.S. would be no more dangerous than background levels. He didn't whip up fear—he dissolved it.

During the early days of the AIDS epidemic, he brought in experts and patients to explain what the disease was, how it worked, and who was truly at risk. He gave truth a stage, not hysteria.

And in the now-infamous interview with Al Campanis, the Dodgers executive who openly made racist comments on live television, Koppel handled it with unshakable professionalism.

He didn't pounce. He didn't spin. He let Campanis speak for himself (even giving him multiple chances to retract himself)—and the world saw the truth without editorializing.

Ted Koppel was an ethical fortress in an increasingly compromised profession.

He covered the most volatile decades in modern American history—from Carter to Biden—and never lost his balance. He was the anti-bluster, the anti-shock, the anti-ego.

He didn't care about ratings. He aired opposite *The Tonight Show* with Johnny Carson, the most-watched nightly show of all time. And he knew he'd never win in viewership. But he didn't care.

He once said:

"We knew the people who needed the news would find us."

And they did. Night after night. For three decades.

Koppel wasn't perfect. But he was ethical to a fault. He believed that journalism should serve the public—not scare it, flatter it, or manipulate it. He trained generations of journalists—by example, not by lecture.

Even today, he laments the state of modern media. He's criticized the Washington Post and New York Times for becoming politically charged. He's sparred with Bill O'Reilly, calling him a threat to objective journalism. And he's spoken, again and again, about the death of the ethical newsroom.

Koppel didn't scream. He didn't market himself. He didn't ride controversy into fame.

He simply showed up, every night, for decades—and told the truth.

Not his truth. *The* truth.

The punchline?

In a world of hot takes and loud voices, Ted Koppel whispered—and people listened.

That's not a style. That's a standard.

That's Ted Koppel.

Chapter 35

Adam Sandler

The Laid-Back Billionaire in Basketball Shorts and XXXL T-Shirts

The Stereotype

Hollywood moguls are image-obsessed. They wear Italian suits, fly private, drink rare champagne, and demand to be seen. They move through red carpets like royalty. Their wealth isn't quiet—it's loud, sharp, and exclusive. And if they do appear modest, it's just PR. A costume of humility. The truth is, power dresses the part.

The Reality

Enter Adam Sandler (1966-Present). Actor. Writer. Producer. Comedian. A Hollywood mogul worth close to $1 billion—and he still dresses like he's on his way to middle school gym class.

Obliterating a Stereotype

We're used to casual fashion now. Athleisure has taken over. Streetwear is mainstream. But 30 years ago, if you saw a grown man wearing long basketball shorts, an oversized superhero T-shirt, and $9.99 Target sneakers, you didn't think "billionaire". You thought: "This guy just got cut from the JV team."

But that was Sandler. And it always has been.

Born in Brooklyn, raised in Manchester, New Hampshire, he came from a working-class family. No pedigree. No spotlight. Just jokes, tenacity, and a refusal to pretend.

He started in stand-up comedy, made his way to Saturday Night Live, and exploded onto the scene with a string of iconic films such as *Billy Madison, Happy Gilmore, Big Daddy, The Waterboy* and several others.

And he did it all while dressing like a slacker on spring break.

But here's the kicker:

It wasn't just a look.

It was a philosophy.

Sandler has said:

> "I wear what I wear because I'm comfortable, and I don't care what anyone thinks."

He never played the Hollywood game. He never ran for awards. He never put on the suit—because he didn't need to.

And while others chased fame, he built a career around fun, friendship, and freedom. He created Happy Madison Productions, wrote and produced his own films, and gave jobs to his closest friends—again and again.

You may not love every Adam Sandler movie. But they're always his movies. And they've made him richer than most studio heads... all while dressing like someone who just doesn't care.

The beauty of Adam Sandler is that he didn't just succeed despite the way he looked. He succeeded because he never cared how he looked.

He didn't sell us status. He sold us comfort, joy, and self-confidence. And in a world of plastic smiles and curated brands, that was revolutionary.

There are no scandals. No meltdowns. No egomania. Just basketball shorts, dad jokes, and an empire built on being the realest guy in the room.

He was mentored by world-class comedian Rodney Dangerfield, who famously said:

> "This kid's gonna own his own company someday."

He was right. Sandler surpassed nearly every comedian of his era—while dressing like he had nothing to prove. And maybe that's the secret.

The punchline?

Adam Sandler is a billionaire in Target shorts—and he doesn't need your respect, because he already earned it.

That's not laziness. That's power in its most relaxed form.

That's Adam Sandler.

Chapter 36

Neil Armstrong

The Greatest Achievement, the Quietest Man

The Stereotype

Those who achieve greatness wear it like armor. They boast. They write memoirs. They sign book deals. They go on talk shows. They remind us—again and again—of what they've done. After all, if you've done the impossible, why not flaunt it? Think of Muhammad Ali: *"It's not bragging if you can back it up."* Think of Napoleon, who crowned himself emperor. Think of Steve Jobs. Elon Musk. General Patton. Richard Branson. History is full of those who turned their achievements into altars to themselves.

The Reality

Enter Neil Armstrong (1930-2012)—a naval aviator, a test pilot, an astronaut, and the first human being to set foot on another world. On July 20, 1969, he took that *"one small step for [a] man, one giant leap for mankind."* And then—he stepped back.

Obliterating a Stereotype

It is perhaps the most famous moment in the history of human exploration. More than Columbus crossing the Atlantic. More than Hillary on Everest. More than Lindbergh crossing the Atlantic solo... perhaps more than all of them together. Armstrong stood on the Sea of Tranquility, 238,900 miles from home, looked up at the blue marble that held all of human history—and said... nothing more. No boasting. No victory speech. No me-first proclamation.

And he meant it.

He did not claim the moonwalk as a personal achievement. He never referred to himself as a hero. When asked about his role in the mission, Armstrong repeatedly said he was simply:

> *"A white-socks, pocket-protector, nerdy engineer who was honored to be involved."*

He called himself a "delivery man"—his job, he explained, was to deliver the spacecraft and its crew to the moon and return it safely. The glory, he said, belonged to the 400,000 NASA engineers, scientists, programmers, welders, mathematicians, seamstresses, and mission control officers who made the Apollo 11 mission possible.

In his own words:

> *"I was just one part of the puzzle."*

He didn't write an autobiography. He didn't go on an endless lecture tour. He declined most interviews. He avoided politics. He refused to make money off his fame. When others cashed in, Armstrong declined—again and again.
1. He refused endorsement deals worth millions.
2. He never signed merchandise.
3. He sued to prevent people from exploiting his name.
4. He quietly taught aerospace engineering at the University of Cincinnati.
5. He later served on the board of Chrysler and quietly advised NASA—but avoided public spectacle.

His silence was not an affectation. It was his nature.

When Neil Armstrong was selected as mission commander for Apollo 11, he didn't ask "why me?" He asked how he could do the job perfectly. That was his standard. He had grown up in Wapakoneta, Ohio—a small-town Midwesterner raised on hard work, humility, and doing things right.

As a test pilot at Edwards Air Force Base, he had already done what most thought was impossible—flying the X-15 at the edge of space. He once saved a NASA mission by overriding the Lunar Module's guidance system and landing it manually with just 15 seconds of fuel remaining. Even then, he barely mentioned it.

Buzz Aldrin, his lunar companion, went on to become a fixture in the media. Armstrong withdrew. He believed the moment was not about him, but about us. That's why his name is less known than the phrase "one small step"—because the message mattered more than the man.

In his rare interviews, he would often turn the conversation toward teamwork, engineering, or mathematics. In his last years, he lived quietly, rarely seen, in the Midwest. He died in 2012.

When he passed, President Obama said:

> "Neil was among the greatest of American heroes—not just of his time, but of all time."

But Armstrong himself would never have accepted the word hero.

He was, in a real sense, a man of duty. Not glory. Not ego. Not performance. And that is what breaks the stereotype most of all. Neil Armstrong stood farther from Earth than any human in history. And yet, no one ever stood with less self-importance.

In a world where humility is rare, and where even small achievements are magnified with self-promotion, Armstrong walked on the moon—and quietly walked away.

Perhaps no one has ever done so much—and said so little about it.

And that's exactly why his greatness endures.

That's Neil Armstrong.

Chapter 37

Mahatma Gandhi

The Revolutionary Who Defeated an Empire Without Firing a Shot

Gandhi, the peaceful revolutionary, leading thousands of people in the 240 mile Salt March, 1930.

The Stereotype

Revolutions are born in blood. They are the product of warfare, guerrilla tactics, and sheer brute force. From the American Revolution to the Russian, from the French to the Irish, from the Visigoths against the Roman Empire to the anti-colonial uprisings in Africa, revolutions are associated with violence, chaos, and military strategy. A revolutionary, by stereotype, is someone who picks up a rifle, takes to the battlefield, and fights for freedom—often to the death.

The Reality

Enter Mohandas Karamchand Gandhi (1869-1948), known to the world as Mahatma Gandhi—the Great Soul. A lawyer by training. A philosopher by discipline. A revolutionary by necessity. The man who defeated the most powerful empire in human history not with bullets or blades, but with silence, sandals, and salt. He led the largest nonviolent revolution ever witnessed—freeing over 300 million people in India, and indirectly another 300 million in Pakistan and Bangladesh, from the grip of the British Empire.

Obliterating a Stereotype

Gandhi defied every convention of what it meant to revolt. The British had held India for generations, under direct rule—first through the East India Company, and later, under the Crown—with an iron fist. India was the jewel of the British Empire, and the colony most tightly gripped by colonial power. The viceroy answered directly to the king. The Indian people were second-class citizens in their own land. And the British had shown no mercy in putting down resistance—whether in Ireland, South Africa, Kenya, or the Caribbean.

Against such a brutal colonial machine, the idea of peaceful resistance seemed absurd. But Gandhi understood something deeper—something almost mystical. He called it Satyagraha—"truth-force." The idea was simple but radical: that moral authority, if rooted in nonviolence and truth, could expose the injustice of violence itself.

And he proved it. Through:

1. The Salt March of 1930, where he walked 240 miles to the Arabian Sea to make salt, defying the British monopoly.
2. The Quit India Movement of 1942, a mass civil disobedience campaign to expel the British.

3. Years of hunger strikes, in which he demanded unity between Hindus and Muslims, and nonviolence in the face of oppression.

Gandhi was arrested many times. He was beaten. He was vilified. But he never retaliated. He never struck back. He never allowed a single drop of blood to stain his movement.

As he famously said:

"An eye for an eye makes the whole world blind."

And:

"First they ignore you, then they laugh at you, then they fight you, then you win."

The British Empire, at its height, ruled nearly a quarter of the world's population and controlled over 26% of the world's land. But Gandhi and his followers brought it to its knees—not with warfare, but with mass refusal. Millions of Hindustanis stopped cooperating. They boycotted British goods, refused to pay taxes, filled the jails, and demonstrated again and again.

It wasn't just political resistance—it was spiritual, cultural, and moral. Gandhi wore simple homespun clothes to reject British textiles. He lived in an ashram, walked barefoot, and insisted on simplicity. He made himself the embodiment of humility and self-discipline. And the more they attacked him, the more the world listened.

Even Winston Churchill, the fiercest defender of empire, could not stop the tide. Churchill reportedly referred to Gandhi as a "half-naked fakir." But even he understood that the loss of India would mark the symbolic end of the British Empire.

And it did. India's independence in 1947—achieved almost entirely without violence—marked the unraveling of the British colonial system. It was the beginning of the end.

Gandhi's legacy transcends India.

1. Martin Luther King Jr. said that Gandhi was the "guiding light" for the American civil rights movement.
2. Nelson Mandela called him "the sacred warrior."
3. The global peace movement, nonviolent protests, and civil resistance around the world—from Eastern Europe to Latin America—are directly descended from his example.

Of course, Gandhi was not without fault. His personal views on certain social matters have been criticized. But none of that changes the reality of what he accomplished: the largest and most successful nonviolent revolution in history.

He didn't just break the stereotype of the revolutionary. He redefined the entire concept of what a revolution could be.

In a world that believed only violence could overcome oppression, Mahatma Gandhi proved otherwise.

And because of him, billions of people today live in nations that exist thanks to peaceful resistance.

He was the man who said no to violence—and won.

And perhaps no one else in history has shattered a stereotype quite like that.

That's Mahatma Gandhi.

Chapter 38

George Washington

The Would-Be Emperor Who Said No to the Throne

The Stereotype

Power is seductive. Power is permanent. People don't walk away from power. When given the opportunity to become emperor, president-for-life, supreme commander, dictator—whatever title—it's always taken. Power corrupts, as the saying goes, and absolute power corrupts absolutely. Once someone has it, they never let it go.

The Reality

Enter George Washington (1732-1799), the American general who had the chance to become king, emperor, or dictator of the United States—and said no. He turned away from the throne not for the love of a woman, not for some personal gain elsewhere, but for righteousness. He walked away because he believed that power belonged to the people, not to one man. And in doing so, he set in motion the model for the modern democratic world.

Obliterating A Stereotype

When we talk about who created the United States, there are many names that come to mind—Thomas Jefferson, James Madison, Alexander Hamilton—men who drafted the theory and the documents of the new republic. But the man who enacted that republic, the one who made it real, who made it work, was George Washington.

Washington led a ragtag army of volunteers to victory against the British Empire, one of the most powerful military forces in history. He was not a military prodigy. He was not the greatest tactician. But he was an extraordinary leader. He held the fragile Continental Army together through cold, starvation, and loss—and he won.

And after winning, he was offered everything. Many of his men wanted him to declare himself king of the United States. He could have taken it. In fact, most people in world history would have taken it. The model was well established: once you win a revolution, you crown yourself ruler. Napoleon did it. Julius Caesar did it. Lenin did it. The Empire of Brazil was formed this way. So was the First Mexican Empire. Across history, revolution simply replaced one crown with another.

But not George Washington.

After his service in the war, he resigned his commission and went home. And after serving two terms as the first President of the United States—he could have run again, and again, and again—he refused. He stepped down voluntarily and walked away. No coups. No riots. Just a citizen returning to private life.

When King George III of Britain heard of Washington's resignation, he is said to have remarked, *"If he does that, he will be the greatest man in the world."*

And that's exactly what Washington did.

He could have been America's king. Instead, he chose to be its example.

That single act—leaving office voluntarily—set the most powerful precedent in modern history: that leaders in a free country are not rulers for life. They are servants of the people. Power is borrowed, not owned. It must be returned.

It was because of George Washington that:

1. The United States became the first modern republic with peaceful transfers of power.
2. Presidents now serve term limits.
3. Independence movements began across the Americas, including Haiti, Mexico, Argentina, Colombia, and eventually even Canada, which gained full legislative independence in 1982 after over a century of gradually becoming independent.

4. The world saw that democracy wasn't just theory—it could work.

Washington did all of this not because he wanted glory. He had already achieved glory. He did it because he believed in the idea of a republic. His words and actions carried more weight than anyone's in his time—but he used them with humility.

He refused a third term. He refused the title of king. He refused to hold on to power.

He gave the world something it had never seen before: a revolutionary who won—and walked away.

George Washington may be the single greatest stereotype buster in history. Because while others clung to power, he let go—and in doing so, gave power back to the people.

That's George Washington.

Chapter 39

Colonel Sanders

The Old Man Who Achieved Success Nearing Age 70

Colonel Sanders, by Norman Rockwell.

The Stereotype

Once you reach retirement age, your time is up. Success is a young man's game. If you haven't made it by 40—or at the latest, 50—then it's never going to happen. You're "too old to start," too slow to adapt, and too set in your ways to build something new.

The Reality

Enter Colonel Harland Sanders (1890-1980). At age 65—broke, alone, and with nothing but a $105 Social Security check—he hit the road in a beat-up car with a white suit, a pressure cooker, and a fried chicken recipe. He knocked on door after door of restaurant after restaurant for two years straight offering to franchise his chicken. He heard "no" 1,009 times before he finally got his first "yes" at age 67. The rest is history: KFC now has over 24,000 restaurants in more than 145 countries, and Colonel Sanders is one of the most recognizable business icons in the world.

Obliterating a Stereotype

In our era of youth obsession, the elderly are routinely sidelined. The culture suggests they are out of touch, incapable of innovation, and best left to rest. The message is clear: if you haven't made it by a certain age, you never will.

But Harland Sanders is living dynamite against that myth. He didn't just "start late"—he started when most people are winding down, moving to Sun Belt communities and reminiscing about the past. At 65 years old, Sanders wasn't reminiscing. He was building.

And his was no overnight success. It took thousands of rejections, two years on the road, sleeping in his car, cooking in parking lots for restaurant owners, and listening to them say "no thank you" over and over and over again. But he didn't stop.

Because he knew what he had. And more importantly, he knew who he was.

When he finally got that first "yes," it changed everything. His system of franchising and his insistence on product consistency allowed his empire to expand fast. He sold the company for $2 million in 1964—about $20 million in today's money—but remained its figurehead until the day he died. His image remains the face of KFC to this day, long after his passing.

But Colonel Sanders wasn't just a fast-food icon—he was a timing icon. He is proof that you are never too old to begin, and that the second half of your life can be more explosive and transformative than the first.

He changed the course of fast-food history. He redefined franchising. And he did it without formal business education, without a big break, and without the "head start" most people believe they need.

He did it at 67.

Stereotype: obliterated.

That's Colonel Sanders.

Chapter 40

Dr. Phil

The Sensitive Southern Psychologist

The Stereotype

Southern men — especially big, drawl-speaking, football-playing men from oil country — aren't supposed to talk about their feelings. They're rough. They're hard. They're no-nonsense types who "tell it like it is," because, to them, sensitivity is weakness. They drink black coffee, quote their grandfathers, and don't have time for therapeutic talk. They're not interested in nuance. They're not interested in vulnerability. They're interested in shutting down nonsense, moving forward, and keeping their boots on the ground. Psychology? That's for rich city folk.

The Reality

Enter Dr. Phil McGraw (1950-Present) — a Southern man to his core. Born in the tiny town of Vinita, Oklahoma (population: just over 5,000), raised in oil-country Kansas and later in Texas, and tough as they come. A former college football linebacker, he earned a scholarship to the University of Tulsa, where he played middle linebacker — and at one point suffered a 100–6 loss to the University of Houston, and kept coming back. Standing at 6'4", with a bald head, a commanding presence, and a booming Texas drawl, he looks every bit the part of a man who would shout you off his porch with shotgun in hand. And yet, that man became one of the most prominent psychologists and counselors of empathy in the world. Not just a therapist, but a PhD-level clinical psychologist, with a master's and doctorate in psychology from the University of North Texas. And beyond that, he became a household name — not for dispensing cold discipline, but for offering help, vulnerability, and a listening ear to millions.

Obliterating a Stereotype

Dr. Phil McGraw launched to national prominence through *The Oprah Winfrey Show*, where his grounded, take-no-BS style struck a nerve. It wasn't therapy laced with jargon. It was therapy laced with honesty — direct but never cruel, firm but never mocking. He cut through people's delusions with tough love, but also deep compassion. He asked hard questions, but he listened to hard answers.

When "Dr. Phil" debuted in 2002, it became the most successful new talk show launch in over a decade — not because he was a shock jock, but because he was the opposite: a calm, strong voice that made people feel heard. For over 20 years and nearly 4,000 episodes, he provided insight into trauma, addiction, family dysfunction, bullying, eating disorders, and emotional pain — and he did it not from an ivory tower, but from the voice of a Southern dad who understood struggle and told you he was on your side.

He didn't shed his Southern identity. He embodied it. But he expanded what it could mean.

Dr. Phil proved that you could be a Southern man, a tough man, a man's man — and still show deep emotional intelligence, vulnerability, and genuine care for others.

And perhaps that's the greatest subversion of the stereotype. Because Dr. Phil didn't reject toughness. He just redefined it. He showed that the toughest thing of all might just be facing your past, admitting your flaws, and doing the work to change.

He's not just a stereotype breaker. He's a bridge. A cultural connector between toughness and tenderness. Between linebacker and therapist. Between Southern grit and emotional grace.

That's Dr. Phil. - The sensitive Southern psychologist.

Chapter 41

Henry Ford

The Farmer Who Changed the World Forever

The Stereotype

Farmers are simple folk. They tend their crops, manage their animals, fix broken tools, and mind their land. They are practical but unimaginative. They are doers, not thinkers. They may be hard-working, but they're certainly not innovators — much less revolutionary world-changers.

The Reality

Enter Henry Ford (1863-1947), raised on a farm in rural Michigan, son of an Irish immigrant, who grew up fixing watches and building machines to make his chores easier. A man with no formal higher education, Ford began life as an ordinary Midwestern farmer — and went on to change human civilization more than perhaps any other individual in modern history.

Obliterating A Stereotype

Ford didn't invent the car. That credit goes to Karl Benz. He didn't invent the assembly line either. But he did take both and push them to a level of perfection, scale, and societal consequence that no one else had imagined. He mass-produced the automobile, turning it from an exotic toy of the rich into an essential tool of the working man. With that single transformation, he didn't just revolutionize transportation — he created the modern age.

But Ford's genius wasn't just mechanical. It was systemic. He understood that producing a single car was less important than reliably producing thousands — and doing so cheaply, efficiently, and consistently. By refining the moving assembly line, he launched the concept of modern mass production, which now defines virtually every product in your home.

But perhaps his most staggering revolution wasn't in machinery — it was in labor policy.

1. In 1914, he shocked the world by doubling worker pay to $5 a day (about 161 dollars in todays terms).
2. In 1914, he introduced the five-day workweek — two days off instead of one.
3. He standardized the eight-hour day, reducing the norm of 10-14 hour shifts.
4. He created the concept of employee wellness and workplace dignity, not out of charity, but because he understood that happy, healthy workers built better machines.

In other words, the modern work-life balance begins with Henry Ford.

But Ford's impact went far beyond his factory. He restructured American society. Before Ford, mobility belonged to the rich. After Ford, every family could dream of owning a car. The Model T democratized motion, and with it, the economy expanded, suburbs grew, the national highway system emerged, fast food chains sprouted, and American individualism took literal form in a steering wheel.

And he didn't come from Yale. Or Harvard. Or inherited wealth. He came from a farm.
He didn't climb the ladder. He built the ladder.

And in that, he obliterated the stereotype that the working class cannot think big.

Henry Ford was not without flaws. His well-documented antisemitism and eccentric social views tarnish aspects of his legacy. But the scale of his influence is beyond dispute. Ford didn't just build cars. He built a blueprint for the industrial world — for how we work, how we produce, how we consume, how we move, and how we live.

He never forgot his roots. He never pretended to be a king or a conqueror. He believed that common men, given the right tools, could do uncommon things. And he proved it.

Henry Ford, the farmer who reshaped the human condition, isn't just a stereotype breaker — he may be the alpha of them all.

That's Henry Ford.

Chapter 42

Ian Anderson

The Rock Star of Temperance

The Stereotype

Rock stars are party animals. They thrive on excess. Their world is a cocktail of sex, drugs, and rock and roll—a whirlwind of backstage debauchery, trashed hotel rooms, late nights, early deaths, and a string of burnt-out guitars, friendships, and livers. If you're not lighting your career on fire while dancing in the flames, are you even really a rock star?

The Reality

Enter Ian Anderson (1947-Present), founder, composer, frontman, flautist, and eternal soul of Jethro Tull, one of the most celebrated progressive rock bands of the 20th century. Emerging in the late 1960s, Jethro Tull stood among giants—Led Zeppelin, Pink Floyd, The Rolling Stones, The Who, The Doors, Cream, and Genesis—bands that didn't just make music; they built the mythos of rock stardom. But Anderson was cut from a different cloth. While his peers overdosed, flamed out, got divorced five times, and built mansions only to lose them in court, Ian Anderson lived like a focused, business-minded artist, with his feet on the ground and a flute in hand. He didn't do drugs. He barely drank. He stayed monogamous. He invested in real estate and salmon farms, not in lines of coke or whiskey brands. And he never, not once, spiraled into the vortex that consumed so many of his generation.

Obliterating A Stereotype

This was the 1960s—the zenith of hedonism in modern culture. The explosion of free love, acid trips, and existential lyrics, where it wasn't just expected for rock stars to push boundaries—it was a requirement. And many paid the price:

1. Jimi Hendrix, Janis Joplin, and Jim Morrison all dead by 27.
2. Keith Moon of The Who, lost in the fog of pills and alcohol.

3. Freddie Mercury, whose nightlife was the stuff of legend and tragedy.
4. Sid Vicious, Bon Scott, Brian Jones—the list is almost endless.

But Ian Anderson kept playing.

With Jethro Tull, he crafted complex, layered compositions—a mix of British folk, classical baroque, and hard rock. His lyrics were sharp, poetic, philosophical. His performances were theatrical. His band's albums—from *Aqualung* to *Thick as a Brick*, from *Songs from the Wood* to *Heavy Horses*—were not about partying. They were about ideas.

Unlike most rock stars, Anderson treated his music career like a vocation. When the checks came in, he didn't buy 10 Bentleys. He bought property. He ran a successful salmon farming business in Scotland for decades. He managed his own finances. He reinvested in his band and his craft. He treated music like work, not escapism.

And that's what makes him so rare.
He is still working.
Still touring – seven decades in.
Still releasing albums.
Still speaking with clarity and calmness on music, politics, and the state of the world.

No scandals. No rehab. No comebacks—because he never fell.

Ian Anderson didn't just write songs. He created a path for rock musicians who didn't want to die at 27 or lose it all by 40. He showed that you could be experimental, bold, theatrical, and iconic without ever sacrificing your self-respect. His flute solos, his eccentric stage presence, his wild-eyed grin—he was weird in the best way, and he did it with a clear head.

Ian Anderson is the ultimate stereotype destroyer in rock history—proof that in a world of chaos, the quiet man with the flute and the business plan can play for eight decades and never miss a note.

That's Ian Anderson.

Chapter 43

Rowan Atkinson

The Electrical Engineer Who Made the World Laugh Without Saying a Word

Rowan Atkinson as his quintessential character, Mr. Bean

The Stereotype

Engineers are dry, introverted figures buried in technical jargon, soldering wires in solitude. They live in the background. They don't smile, and they certainly don't make you laugh.

Meanwhile, comedians are the opposite: loud, energetic, manic showmen who are desperate for attention. They speak in fast rhythms, build punchlines, riff, roast, and banter. Above all, they talk.

The Reality

Enter Rowan Atkinson (1955-Present) — Oxford-educated electrical engineer, owner of a master's degree from The Queen's College and the silent comedic genius behind Mr. Bean, the most universally beloved comedy character of the 20th century... a man who made the whole world laugh without ever saying a word.

Obliterating A Stereotype

Born in 1955 in Consett, County Durham, England, Atkinson was the youngest of four brothers. His early life was a quiet one. And yes, he did have a stutter — not a dramatic speech impediment, but enough that he found freedom in physical performance far more than in verbal sparring. While studying electrical engineering at Newcastle University and later at Oxford, he began writing and performing sketches for comedy troupes, eventually making waves at the Edinburgh Fringe Festival.

But here's where Atkinson breaks not just one, but two massive stereotypes:

1. **The Silent Comedian:** Mr. Bean, the bumbling, rubber-faced man-child Atkinson created in 1989, speaks no real language — just murmurs and the occasional grunt. And yet the character became one of the most internationally recognized comedic icons of all time. Mr. Bean is essentially Buster Keaton meets Charlie Chaplin in the body of an Oxford academic. His silent physical comedy bypassed language barriers entirely. The result? Mr. Bean has been broadcast in nearly 200 countries, translated without effort into every culture, and watched

by over 300 million people per episode during its peak. This wasn't just popular comedy. This was global dominion through pantomime.

2. **The Laughing Engineer:** Atkinson's technical education never disappeared. He once described acting as a form of engineering — breaking scenes into parts, controlling physical movement like a machine, rehearsing with obsessive precision. He is famously fastidious, logical, and intensely private. While most comedians live chaotic lives, Atkinson is exacting, organized, and brilliant — the perfect mind to create surgical physical comedy that relies on millimeter-perfect timing.

He also loves fast cars, races them semi-professionally, and has written detailed essays on car performance in CAR Magazine. Again: not your typical stand-up comic.

Mr. Bean may look like a childish idiot in a brown tweed jacket, but behind that silent mask was a man who applied the rigor of engineering to create a universal comedy language.

And that's exactly what Rowan Atkinson accomplished. In a world where comedians shout and engineers are quiet, he flipped the paradigm. The engineer became the funniest man in the world — and he did it without saying a damn word.

That's Rowan Atkinson.

Chapter 44

Harry S. Truman
The Everyman President

The Stereotype

Presidents are larger-than-life. They're orators, icons, symbols, and statues in the making. They walk with gravity, speak with thunder, and live with the belief that they are history incarnate. Think FDR and his patrician authority. Think JFK's Camelot. Think Teddy Roosevelt and his truly out-of-this world presence.

Think Reagan's stagecraft, or Trump's omnipresence. Around the world, from Caesars to Tsars, from Emperors to modern presidents, the leader is a brand, an ego, a monument.

The Reality

Enter Harry S. Truman. 33rd President of the United States. A man with no charisma, no dynasty, no grandeur. Just quiet discipline, moral courage, and an unwavering sense of duty. He wasn't elected president—he inherited the office after Franklin D. Roosevelt's sudden death in April 1945. He had been vice president for just 82 days. He had been largely ignored by the Roosevelt administration. And then—he became the most powerful man in the world, at the most critical moment in the history of the world.

Obliterating a Stereotype

Harry Truman was born in Lamar, Missouri in 1884.

He worked as:
1. A farmer
2. A bank clerk
3. A failed haberdasher (a men's clothing shop owner)

He never even earned a college degree. He read voraciously. He studied history, Latin, the classics—on his own.

He once said:

> *"Not all readers are leaders, but all leaders are readers."*

When he moved into the White House after FDR's death, he brought one truckload of personal belongings. FDR's family had left with 50 truckloads. That contrast says everything.

But that was only a tiny example of who he was.

Truman walked alone through Washington, while in Office. He refused extended Secret Service protection after his presidency ended. He lived in the same house with his wife Bess—the only woman he ever dated—until his death. He wrote his own letters, carried his own bags, and never hired a speechwriter. His handwriting—small, neat, frugal—matched his life.

But don't let the humility fool you.
This was the man who:

1. Authorized the dropping of the atomic bombs on Hiroshima and Nagasaki
2. Ended World War II
3. Recognized the state of Israel
4. Implemented the Marshall Plan, rebuilding Europe
5. Created NATO
6. Was instrumental in creating the United Nations Organization
7. Desegregated the U.S. military
8. Fired General MacArthur—a global celebrity and hero of World War II—for insubordination
9. And laid the groundwork for modern American foreign policy in the Cold War

He didn't want power. But he wielded it with unflinching clarity.

When his presidency ended in 1953, he went home to Independence, Missouri. No corporate boards. No memoir advance. No presidential library vanity tour. Just a man in a hat, walking to the drugstore.

He refused to cash in on the presidency. He lived on his Army pension—just $112 a month—until Congress passed the Former Presidents Act in 1958, largely because of his financial modesty.

In a world of political egos, Harry Truman stood alone: He saw leadership not as a brand—but as a burden.

He once said:

"It's amazing what you can accomplish if you do not care who gets the credit."

And he lived that principle, every day.

His right-hand man was General George C. Marshall, another quiet giant. Together, they reshaped the world—without seeking fame, without chasing legacy, without spectacle.

They just worked.

Truman didn't want to be president. But he rose to the occasion. And he did it not by becoming larger-than-life—but by staying exactly who he was:

A reader. A doer. A man who knew when to say yes, and when to walk away.

The punchline? He ended a world war, built a new world order, and went home with no parade.

That's not power. That's character.

That's Harry S. Truman.

Chapter 45

Jimmy Carter

The President Whose Life of Service Began After the Presidency

President Carter overseeing the 1996 Palestinian General election, the first in that country's history, a full 15 years after he had left office.

The Stereotype

Former presidents fade into retirement. They give speeches, paint, publish memoirs, sit on boards, enjoy security, collect honors, and disappear into the soft glow of history. Their work is behind them. Their impact is frozen in office. Once they leave the White House, their relevance expires with the oath.

The Reality

Enter Jimmy Carter. 39th President of the United States. Peanut farmer. Naval officer. Energy engineer. Governor of Georgia. President during the painful stagflation era of the 1970s. And the man who, after leaving the presidency, became the greatest former head of state in world history—by dedicating the next 40 years of his life to peace, justice, human rights, and service.

Obliterating a Stereotype

When Jimmy Carter left office in January 1981, he was 56 years old. He had endured a presidency marred by inflation, the Iran hostage crisis, energy crises, and a painful cultural reckoning. Many called his presidency weak. They were wrong—but history would take time to catch up.

He left the White House without bitterness. Without show. Without cynicism. He returned to Plains, Georgia—to his one-story home, his local church, and his real mission.

Because Jimmy Carter didn't retire. He got to work.

He founded The Carter Center in 1982—an organization dedicated to:

1. Conflict resolution
2. Election monitoring
3. Human rights
4. Public health

Through the Carter Center, he:

1. Monitored over 100 democratic elections in more than 39 countries
2. Mediated conflicts in Haiti, North Korea, Bosnia, Sudan, and the Middle East
3. Helped eradicate Guinea worm disease, reducing cases from 3.5 million to less than a dozen

4. Promoted free and fair elections in Africa, Latin America, and Asia
5. Fought river blindness, malaria, trachoma, and lymphatic filariasis
6. Championed mental health reform, housing rights, and rural education

All of this—after leaving the presidency.

He also built homes with Habitat for Humanity well into his 90s, hammer in hand, side by side with volunteers. He wrote over 30 books—on peace, faith, justice, policy, and memoirs. He taught Sunday school every week at his local church. He refused to profit from his presidency. He never joined corporate boards. He never charged six figures for speeches. He chose mission over money.

He lived in a home worth less than $200,000, drove himself to the grocery store, and insisted on carrying his own luggage when traveling.

In 2002, he was awarded the Nobel Peace Prize—not for his time as president, but for his post-presidency:

"For decades of untiring effort to find peaceful solutions to international conflicts, to advance democracy and human rights, and to promote economic and social development."

No other president nor world leader—none—has ever done more for the world after leaving office.

Carter's presidency, once maligned, has been re-evaluated:

1. He appointed Paul Volcker as Fed Chair, triggering the end of the stagflation era that lasted 15 years and is the second biggest economic crisis in American history, only after the Great Depression.
2. He created the Department of Energy and the Department of Education

3. He put solar panels on the White House
4. He brokered the Camp David Accords, one of the most significant peace agreements in the Middle East
5. He pushed hard for human rights abroad, even when it cost him politically
6. He had a plan for full energy independence of America, involving transitioning fully to synthetic oil.

But all of that now feels like the prologue.

His real impact came after the Oval Office.
When no one was watching.
When no one demanded it.
And he did it anyway.

He didn't retire as a statesman.
He evolved into a global moral force.

The punchline?

Jimmy Carter was a decent president. But he became the greatest ex-president who ever lived.

That's not a footnote.
That's a legacy.

That's Jimmy Carter.

Epilogue

Stereotypes?... Out the Window They Go

If there's one thing I hope you walk away with after reading this book, it's this: stereotypes are not to be trusted. They are meant to be busted. They are not blueprints. They are not bedrock. They are not truths. They're shortcuts—handy if you want to compartmentalize the world, but deeply flawed if you actually want to understand it.

Stereotypes reduce the human experience to laziness. They strip people of dimension. They turn vibrant lives into stick figures. Yes, some people do fit their stereotype. But many—many others—do not. And those are the ones this book was written for.

I want you to understand that Ross Perot was not the only tech mogul with a Southern twang. That Barry Goldwater wasn't the only far-right conservative who was pro-choice, pro-LGBT, pro-feminism, pro-drug policy reform, and pro-civil rights. That Cory Everson isn't the only muscular woman who radiates femininity. That Steve Reeves wasn't the only Herculean man who preferred modesty. That Arnold Schwarzenegger isn't the only muscle-bound polymath. That Paul Kruger wasn't the only leader who designed an anti-government government. That F.W. de Klerk wasn't the only dictator who dismantled his own dictatorship. That George Washington wasn't the only man to walk away from a throne he could have kept.

The world is full of stereotype busters. Maybe you're one yourself.

And that's the most important thing of all: we must stop reducing people to caricatures. We must stop assuming that one data point defines a life. Sure, it's easier that way. Sure, it's comforting. But it isn't the truth. And it isn't how life is meant to be lived.

When you begin to break stereotypes, something happens—you become more dimensional yourself. You become sharper, kinder, wiser. You stop accepting single-serving stories and start seeing the full meal.

If your only taste of lasagna comes from a cold airplane tray, and you've never had real lasagna before, you might believe that's all there is. You'll make a judgment—and you'll be wrong. Stereotypes are cold airplane lasagna. They are the leftovers of lazy thinking. And they rob us of the richness of the world.

So, break them.
Strive for depth.
Look twice.
Think again.

That's what this book was about. I hope you enjoyed it.

And as you close this chapter, I ask you to remember: somebody out there will make assumptions about you. You know they're wrong. They don't know your story. They're just filling in the gaps with what's easy. So instead of trying to disprove them, try this:

Disprove yourself.

Catch yourself assuming things about others. Challenge it. Question it. Replace it with curiosity.

And when you lay your head down tonight, think of someone—someone who isn't in this book—who breaks a stereotype in their own quiet or wild way. Keep your eyes open for them. They're out there.

Until next time.

Happy hunting, good luck, and best wishes.
—Dr. Robbie King

Copyrights of Images

1. Chapter 1: Image of Bill Murray, part of Public Domain.
2. Chapter 2: Image of F.W. De Klerk and Nelson Mandela. This file is licensed under the Creative Commons Attribution-Share Alike 2.0 Generic license. Link to the license available here. creativecommons.org/licenses/by-sa/2.0/deed.en
3. Chapter 3: Image of Tom Selleck. Image rights purchased from Alamy. License: Standard, Individual Pack. Photograph by Pictorial Press. License terms: Individual License for 1 user only. Allowed usage: across websites and social media, short-form-video on video sharing sites, digital publishing, digital marketing, print runs of up to 5,000 for print marketing and self-published book.
4. Chapter 4: Image of Dr. Hugo Eckener on White House lawn, with president Calvin Coolidge, part of Public Domain.
5. Chapter 5: Image of Ross Perot in 1992 Presidential debate, part of Public Domain.
6. Chapter 6: Image of Barry Goldwater, part of Public Domain.
7. Chapter 7: Image of Paul Kruger, part of Public Domain.
8. Chapter 8: Image of Bill Goldberg. Image rights purchased from Alamy. License: Standard, Individual Pack. Photograph by ZUMA. License terms: Individual License for 1 user only. Allowed usage: across websites and social media, short-form-video on video sharing sites, digital publishing, digital marketing, print runs of up to 5,000 for print marketing and self-published book.
9. Chapter 9: Image of Rick Harrison, speaking at the 2018 Conservative Political Action Conference (CPAC) in National Harbor, Maryland. Photo by Gage Skidmore from Peoria, AZ, United States of America. This file is licensed under the Creative Commons Attribution-Share Alike 2.0

Generic license. Link to the license available here. creativecommons.org/licenses/by-sa/2.0/deed.en

10. Chapter 10: Image of Albert Schweitzer, in Lambarene 1964 (By Gert Chesi). This file is licensed under the Creative Commons Attribution-Share Alike 4.0 International license. Link to the license available here. creativecommons.org/licenses/by-sa/4.0/deed.en
11. Chapter 11: Image of Steve Martin, by Jim Summaria, circa 1977. This file is is licensed under the Creative Commons Attribution-Share Alike 3.0 Unported license. Link to the license available here. creativecommons.org/licenses/by-sa/3.0/deed.en
12. Chapter 12: Image of Peter Weller as Robocop. Image rights purchased from Alamy. License: Standard, Individual Pack. License terms: Individual License for 1 user only. Allowed usage: across websites and social media, short-form-video on video sharing sites, digital publishing, digital marketing, print runs of up to 5,000 for print marketing and self-published book.
13. Chapter 13: Image of Elvira (Cassandra Peterson). Image rights purchased from Alamy. License: Standard, Individual Pack. License terms: Individual License for 1 user only. Allowed usage: across websites and social media, short-form-video on video sharing sites, digital publishing, digital marketing, print runs of up to 5,000 for print marketing and self-published book.
14. Chapter 14: Image of Nina Hartley, This photograph was taken by Glenn Francis (User:Toglenn) and released under the license(s) stated below. You are free to use it as long as you credit me and follow the terms of the license. Attribution : © Glenn Francis, www.PacificProDigital.com (Email: glennfrancis@pacificprodigital.com). This file is is licensed under the Creative Commons Attribution-Share Alike 3.0 Unported license. Link to the license available here. creativecommons.org/licenses/by-sa/3.0/deed.en
15. Chapter 15: Image of Corey Everson. Photograph by ZUMA Press. Image rights purchased from Alamy. License: Standard, Individual Pack. License terms:

Individual License for 1 user only. Allowed usage: across websites and social media, short-form-video on video sharing sites, digital publishing, digital marketing, print runs of up to 5,000 for print marketing and self-published book.
16. Chapter 16: Image of Pandora Peaks. Photograph by Moviestore Collection. Image rights purchased from Alamy. License: Standard, Individual Pack. License terms: Individual License for 1 user only. Allowed usage: across websites and social media, short-form-video on video sharing sites, digital publishing, digital marketing, print runs of up to 5,000 for print marketing and self-published book.
17. Chapter 17: Image of James Randi. James Randi demonstrating 'psychic surgery' on the ITV series *James Randi, Psychic Investigator*, made by Open Media in 1991. Photograph by Open Media Ltd. This file is licensed under the Creative Commons Attribution-Share Alike 4.0 International license. Link to the license available here: /creativecommons.org/licenses/by-sa/4.0/deed.en
18. Chapter 18: Image of Rodney Dangerfield. Photograph part of Public Domain.
19. Chapter 19: Image of Tony Danza. Photograph by Moviestore Collection. Image rights purchased from Alamy. License: Standard, Individual Pack. License terms: Individual License for 1 user only. Allowed usage: across websites and social media, short-form-video on video sharing sites, digital publishing, digital marketing, print runs of up to 5,000 for print marketing and self-published book.
20. Chapter 20: Image of Gene Siskel and Roger Ebert. Photograph by PictureLux. Image rights purchased from Alamy. License: Standard, Individual Pack. License terms: Individual License for 1 user only. Allowed usage: across websites and social media, short-form-video on video sharing sites, digital publishing, digital marketing, print runs of up to 5,000 for print marketing and self-published book.

21. Chapter 21: Image of Koos de la Rey. Photograph part of Public Domain.
22. Chapter 22: Image of Isaac Asimov. Photograph part of Public Domain.
23. Chapter 23: Image of John Gierach. Credit: Leehall7. This file is licensed under the Creative Commons Attribution-Share Alike 4.0 International license. Link to the license available here: creativecommons.org/licenses/by-sa/4.0/deed.en
24. Chapter 24: Image of USSR Hockey team beating Canada. Credit: Basch, Fritz, Dutch National Archives, The Hague, Fotocollectie Algemeen Nederlands Persbureau (ANeFo), 1945-1989, Nummer toegang 2.24.01.04 Bestanddeelnummer 920-1920. This file is licensed under the Creative Commons Attribution-Share Alike 3.0 Netherlands license. Link to the license available here: creativecommons.org/licenses/by-sa/3.0/nl/deed.en
25. Chapter 25: Image of Bill James. Credit: Colette Morton and Dan Holden. This file is licensed under the Creative Commons Attribution-Share Alike 2.0 Generic license. Link to the license available here: creativecommons.org/licenses/by-sa/2.0/deed.en
26. Chapter 26: Image of Steve Reeves. Photograph part of Public Domain.
27. Chapter 27: Image of Sam Walton's office. Photograph by Picturelibrary. Image rights purchased from Alamy. License: Standard, Individual Pack. License terms: Individual License for 1 user only. Allowed usage: across websites and social media, short-form-video on video sharing sites, digital publishing, digital marketing, print runs of up to 5,000 for print marketing and self-published book.
28. Chapter 28: Image of George C. Marshall. Photograph part of Public Domain.
29. Chapter 29: Image of Arnold Schwarzenegger. Photograph part of Public Domain.
30. Chapter 30: Image of John Bogle. Credit: Bill Cramer/Wonderful Machine Contact:

connect@wonderfulmachine.com This file is licensed under the Creative Commons Attribution-Share Alike 4.0 International license. Link to the license available here: creativecommons.org/licenses/by-sa/4.0/deed.en

31. Chapter 31: Image of Fred Rogers. Photograph part of Public Domain.
32. Chapter 32: Image of Bob Ross. Photograph part of Public Domain.
33. Chapter 33: Image of Bob Woodward. Photograph part of Public Domain.
34. Chapter 34: Image of Ted Koppel. Photograph part of Public Domain.
35. Chapter 35: Image of Adam Sandler, Photograph by Wenn. Image rights purchased from Alamy. License: Standard, Individual Pack. License terms: Individual License for 1 user only. Allowed usage: across websites and social media, short-form-video on video sharing sites, digital publishing, digital marketing, print runs of up to 5,000 for print marketing and self-published book.
36. Chapter 36: Image of Neil Armstrong. Photograph part of Public Domain.
37. Chapter 37: Image of Mahatma Gandhi. Photograph part of Public Domain.
38. Chapter 38: Image of George Washington. Painting part of Public Domain.
39. Chapter 39: Image of Harlan Sanders. Painting part of Public Domain.
40. Chapter 40: Image of Phil McGraw. This file is licensed under the Creative Commons Attribution-Share Alike 3.0 Unported license. **Attribution: Angela George.** Link to the license available here: creativecommons.org/licenses/by-sa/3.0/deed.en
41. Chatper 41: Image of Henry Ford. Photograph part of Public Domain.
42. Chapter 42: Image of Ian Anderson. Photograph part of Public Domain.
43. Chapter 43: Image of Rowan Atkinson. Photo taken by Gerhard Heeke. Permission is granted to copy, distribute and/or modify this document under the terms

of the **GNU Free Documentation License**, Version 1.2 or any later version published by the Free Software Foundation; with no Invariant Sections, no Front-Cover Texts, and no Back-Cover Texts. Link to the license available here: commons.wikimedia.org/wiki/Commons:GNU_Free_Documentation_License,_version_1.2

44. Chapter 44: Image of Harry S. Truman. Photograph part of Public Domain.
45. Chapter 45: Image of Jimmy Carter. Source, UNRWA: United Nations Relief and Works Agency for Palestine Refugees in the Near East. This file is licensed under the Creative Commons Attribution-Share Alike 4.0 International license. Link to the license available here: creativecommons.org/licenses/by-sa/4.0/deed.en

www.ingramcontent.com/pod-product-compliance
Lightning Source LLC
Chambersburg PA
CBHW030319080526
44584CB00012B/623